... THY GUIDE,
IN THY MOST NEED
TO GO BY THY SIDE

EVERYMAN'S LIBRARY
POCKET POETS

C. P. CAVAFY
POEMS

••••••••••••••••••

SELECTED
WITH TRANSLATION
AND NOTES BY
DANIEL MENDELSOHN

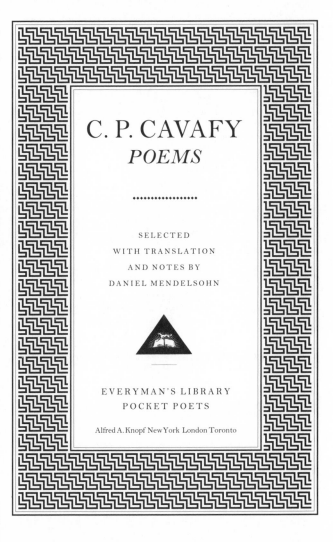

EVERYMAN'S LIBRARY
POCKET POETS

Alfred A. Knopf New York London Toronto

THIS IS A BORZOI BOOK

PUBLISHED BY ALFRED A. KNOPF

This edition first published in Everyman's Library, 2014
Translation and notes copyright © 2009, 2012, 2014 by
Daniel Mendelsohn

Poems in this collection have been selected from *C. P. Cavafy: Collected
Poems* and *C. P. Cavafy: The Unfinished Poems* originally published in
hardcover in the United States by Alfred A. Knopf, a division of Random
House LLC, New York, in 2009, and subsequently published in one revised
volume as *C. P. Cavafy: Complete Poems* by Alfred A. Knopf, a division of
Random House LLC, New York, in 2012.

www.randomhouse.com/everymans
www.everymanslibrary.co.uk

ISBN 978-0-375-71242-5 (US)
978-1-84159-796-6 (UK)

A CIP catalogue record for this book is available from the British Library

Library of Congress Cataloging-in-Publication Data
Cavafy, Constantine, 1863–1933, author.
[Poems. Selections. English]
Poems / by C. P. Cavafy; [translation and notes by Daniel Mendelsohn].
p. cm.—(Everyman's Library pocket poets)
ISBN 978-0-375-71242-5 (hardcover: alk. paper)
I. Title. II. Series: Everyman's Library pocket poets.
PA5610.K2A2 2014   2013045761
889.1′32—dc23

Typography by Peter B. Willberg

Typeset in the UK by AccComputing, Wincanton, Somerset

Printed and bound in Germany by GGP Media GmbH, Pössneck

CONTENTS

PREFACE

Constantine Cavafy was born on April 29, 1863 in Alexandria, the last of seven sons of well-to-do parents who had come to Egypt from Constantinople. The death of his father, when Cavafy was nine, left the family in financial difficulties; for a number of years afterward the widow Cavafy and her younger sons lived, dependent on the generosity of relatives, in England. (It was there that Cavafy acquired the British accent that, we are told, colored his Greek.) The family resettled in Alexandria when Cavafy was fourteen, and with the exception of a three-year sojourn with relations in Constantinople in the 1880s, he lived there for the rest of his life.

In 1892, Cavafy obtained a position with the Ministry of Public Works, in an office with a comically Dantesque name, the "Third Circle of Irrigation"; he remained there until his retirement, thirty years later. At around the same time he began publishing articles and poems in newspapers and literary journals. These early publications already bear witness to a deep, even scholarly interest in all phases of Greek history, from the Classical and Hellenistic periods to Late Antiquity and Byzantium, which would provide the subjects for many of his mature poems. During the same formative period Cavafy lived with his mother, Haricleia, dutifully dining with her most evenings and escaping afterward into the city's homosexual demimonde. This world of furtive yearnings and clandestine encounters would provide him with his other great subject: desire between men.

Eventually Cavafy settled into an antique-crammed apartment on the Rue Lepsius – today the Cavafy Museum – where he would hold forth to friends and guests, in Greek or English or French, on the erudite subjects he cherished: "the tricky behavior of the Emperor Manuel Comnenus in 1096," as his friend E. M. Forster recalled, "or ... olives, their possibilities and price, or ... the fortunes of friends, or George Eliot, or the dialects of the interior of Asia Minor." It is to Forster, whom Cavafy met during World War I in Alexandria, that we owe the most famous description of the idiosyncratic poet: "a Greek gentleman in a straw hat, standing absolutely motionless at a slight angle to the universe."

A lifelong smoker, Cavafy was diagnosed with cancer of the larynx in 1932. After traveling to Athens for treatment that summer, he returned to his beloved Alexandria, where he died the following year, on his seventieth birthday.

* * *

This volume contains selections from all of Cavafy's work. PUBLISHED POEMS consists of selections from the three collections that the poet self-published

(*Poems 1905–1915*, *Poems 1916–1918*, and *Poems 1919–1932*), as well as from the "Sengopoulos Notebook," a selection of poems that he prepared for his friend and heir, Alexander Sengopoulos. The REPUDIATED POEMS are early published verses that Cavafy later disowned. UNPUBLISHED POEMS features finished work that the poet did not wish to publish but which he saved in his files; these were first published in 1968. UNFINISHED POEMS is the designation for the thirty nearly complete drafts that the poet left at the time of his death, edited and published in a scholarly Greek edition in 1994.

In the case of selections from the Published Poems, *italicized* dates at the bottom of each page refer to the year of composition, when known; years in roman type refer to date of original publication. For the Unpublished and Unfinished Poems, the year in brackets at the bottom of the page indicates date of composition, when known.

From
POEMS 1905–1915

THE CITY

You said: "I'll go to some other land, I'll go to some
    other sea.
There's bound to be another city that's better by far.
My every effort has been ill-fated from the start;
my heart – like something dead – lies buried away;
How long will my mind endure this slow decay?
Wherever I look, wherever I cast my eyes,
I see all round me the black rubble of my life
where I've spent so many ruined and wasted years."

You'll find no new places, you won't find other shores.
The city will follow you. The streets in which you pace
will be the same, you'll haunt the same familiar places,
and inside those same houses you'll grow old.
You'll always end up in this city. Don't bother to hope
for a ship, a route, to take you somewhere else;
    they don't exist.
Just as you've destroyed your life, here in this
small corner, so you've wasted it through all the world.

[*1894*; 1910]

THE SATRAPY

What a pity, given that you're made
for deeds that are glorious and great,
that this unjust fate of yours always
leads you on, and denies you your success;
that base habits get in your way,
and pettinesses, and indifference.
How terrible, too, the day when you give in
(the day when you let yourself go and give in),
and leave to undertake the trip to Susa,
and go to the monarch Artaxerxes,
who graciously establishes you at court,
and offers you satrapies, and the like.
And you, you accept them in despair,
these things that you don't want.
But your soul seeks, weeps for other things:
the praise of the People and the Sophists,
the hard-won, priceless "Bravos";
the Agora, the Theatre, and the victors' Crowns.
How will Artaxerxes give you *them*,
how will you find *them* in the satrapy;
and what kind of life, without them, will you live.

20   [*1905*; 1910]

BUT WISE MEN APPREHEND
WHAT IS IMMINENT

The gods perceive what lies in the future, and mortals,
what occurs in the present, but wise men apprehend what
is imminent.

PHILOSTRATUS, *Life of Apollonius of Tyana*, VIII, 7

Mortal men perceive things as they happen.
What lies in the future the gods perceive,
full and sole possessors of all enlightenment.
Of all the future holds, wise men apprehend
what is imminent. Their hearing,

sometimes, in moments of complete
absorption in their studies, is disturbed. The secret call
of events that are about to happen reaches them.
And they listen to it reverently. While in the street
outside, the people hear nothing at all.

[*1896*; 1899; <1915]

IDES OF MARCH

Of glory be you fearful, O my Soul.
And if you are unable to defeat
your ambitions, then hesitantly, guardedly
pursue them. And the further you proceed,
the more searching, the more attentive must you be.

And when at last you reach your apogee – a Caesar;
and cut the figure of someone greatly renowned,
then take heed more than ever as you go out on
    the street,
a man of power, conspicuous with your retinue,
when someone approaches you out of the crowd,
a certain Artemidorus, bringing a letter,
and hurriedly says "Read this right away,
it's something important that concerns you,"
don't fail to stop; don't fail to put off
all talk and business; don't fail to
brush off all and sundry who salute and fawn
(you can see them later); let even
the Senate wait, and find out at once
the weighty contents of Artemidorus's letter.

FINISHED

Deep in fear and in suspicion,
with flustered minds and terrified eyes,
we wear ourselves out figuring how
we might avoid the certain
danger that threatens us so terribly.
And yet we're mistaken, that's not it ahead:
the news was wrong
(or we didn't hear it; or didn't get it right).
But a disaster that we never imagined
suddenly, shatteringly breaks upon us,
and unprepared – no time left now – we are swept away.

[*1910*; 1911]   23

THE GOD ABANDONS ANTONY

When suddenly, at midnight, there comes the sound
of an invisible procession passing by
with exquisite music playing, with voices raised –
your good fortune, which now gives way;
     all your efforts'
ill-starred outcome; the plans you made for life,
which turned out wrong: don't mourn them uselessly.
Like one who's long prepared, like someone brave,
bid farewell to her, to Alexandria, who is leaving.
Above all do not fool yourself, don't say
that it was a dream, that your ears deceived you;
don't stoop to futile hopes like these.
Like one who's long prepared, like someone brave,
as befits a man who's proved worthy of a city like
     this one,
go without faltering toward the window
and listen with deep emotion, but not
with the entreaties and the whining of a coward,
to the sounds – a final entertainment –
to the exquisite instruments of that initiate crew,
and bid farewell to her, to Alexandria, whom you
     are losing.

THEODOTUS

If you are among the truly elect,
watch how you achieve your predominance.
However much you're glorified, however much
your accomplishments in Italy and Thessaly
are blazoned far and wide by governments,
however many honorary decrees
are bestowed on you in Rome by your admirers,
neither your elation nor your triumph will endure,
nor will you feel superior – superior how? –
when, in Alexandria, Theodotus brings you,
upon a charger that's been stained with blood,
poor wretched Pompey's head.

And do not take it for granted that in your life,
restricted, regimented, and mundane,
such spectacular and terrifying things don't exist.
Maybe at this very moment, into some neighbor's
nicely tidied house there comes –
invisible, immaterial – Theodotus,
bringing one such terrifying head.

[<*1911*; 1915]   25

MONOTONY

On one monotone day one more
monotone, indistinct day follows. The same
things will happen, then again recur –
identical moments find us, then go their way.

One month passes bringing one month more.
What comes next is easy enough to know:
the boredom from the day before.
And tomorrow's got to where it seems like no
        tomorrow.

ITHACA

As you set out on the way to Ithaca
hope that the road is a long one,
filled with adventures, filled with discoveries.
The Laestrygonians and the Cyclopes,
Poseidon in his anger: do not fear them,
you won't find such things on your way
so long as your thoughts remain lofty, and a choice
emotion touches your spirit and your body.
The Laestrygonians and the Cyclopes,
savage Poseidon; you won't encounter them
unless you stow them away inside your soul,
unless your soul sets them up before you.

Hope that the road is a long one.
Many may the summer mornings be
when – with what pleasure, with what joy –
you first put in to harbors new to your eyes;
may you stop at Phoenician trading posts
and there acquire the finest wares:
mother-of-pearl and coral, amber and ebony,
and heady perfumes of every kind:
as many heady perfumes as you can.
Many Egyptian cities may you visit
that you may learn, and go on learning, from
        their sages.

Always in your mind keep Ithaca.
To arrive there is your destiny.
But do not hurry your trip in any way.
Better that it last for many years;
that you drop anchor at the island an old man,
rich with all you've gotten on the way,
not expecting Ithaca to make you rich.

Ithaca gave you the beautiful journey;
without her you wouldn't have set upon the road.
But now she has nothing left to give you.

And if you find her poor, Ithaca didn't deceive you.
As wise as you will have become, with so much
        experience,
you will understand, by then, these Ithacas;
        what they mean.

AS MUCH AS YOU CAN

And even if you cannot make your life the way you
        want it,
this much, at least, try to do
as much as you can: don't cheapen it
with too much intercourse with society,
with too much movement and conversation.

Don't cheapen it by taking it about,
making the rounds with it, exposing it
to the everyday inanity
of relations and connections,
so it becomes like a stranger, burdensome.

[*1905*; 1913]

TROJANS

Our efforts, those of the ill-fortuned;
our efforts are the efforts of the Trojans.
We will make a bit of progress; we will start
to pick ourselves up a bit; and we'll begin
to be intrepid, and to have some hope.

But something always comes up, and stops us cold.
In the trench in front of us Achilles
emerges, and affrights us with his shouting. –

Our efforts are the efforts of the Trojans.
We imagine that with resolve and daring
we will reverse the animosity of fortune,
and so we take our stand outside, to fight.

But whenever the crucial moment comes,
our boldness and our daring disappear;
our spirit is shattered, comes unstrung;
and we scramble all around the walls
seeking in our flight to save ourselves.

And yet our fall is certain. Up above,
on the walls, already the lament has begun.
They mourn the memory, the sensibility, of our days.
Bitterly Priam and Hecuba mourn for us.

30   [*1900*; 1905]

KING DEMETRIUS

Not like a king, but like an actor, he exchanged his showy
robe of state for a dark cloak, and in secret stole away.
PLUTARCH, Life of Demetrius

When the Macedonians deserted him,
and made it clear that it was Pyrrhus they preferred
King Demetrius (who had a noble
soul) did not – so they said –
behave at all like a king. He went
and cast off his golden clothes,
and flung off his shoes
of richest purple. In simple clothes
he dressed himself quickly and left:
doing just as an actor does
who, when the performance is over,
changes his attire and departs.

[<i>1900</i>; <i>1906</i>]

THE RETINUE OF DIONYSUS

Damon the artisan (none as fine
as he in the Peloponnese) is
fashioning the Retinue of Dionysus
in Parian marble. The god in his divine
glory leads, with vigor in his stride.
Intemperance behind. Beside
Intemperance, Intoxication pours the Satyrs wine
from an amphora that they've garlanded with vines.
Near them delicate Sweetwine, his eyes
half-closed, mesmerizes.
And further down there come the singers,
Song and Melody, and Festival
who never allows the hallowed processional
torch that he holds to go out. Then, most modest,
        Ritual. –
That's what Damon is making. Along with all
of that, from time to time he gets to pondering
the fee he'll be receiving from the king
of Syracuse, three talents, quite a lot.
When that's added to the money that he's got,
he'll be well-to-do, will lead a life of leisure,
can get involved in politics – what pleasure! –
he too in the Council, he too in the Agora.

32   [*1903*; 1907]

ALEXANDRIAN KINGS

The Alexandrians came out in droves
to have a look at Cleopatra's children:
Caesarion, and also his little brothers,
Alexander and Ptolemy, who for the first
time were being taken to the Gymnasium,
that they might proclaim them kings
before the brilliant ranks of soldiers.

Alexander: they declared him king
of Armenia, of Media, of the Parthians.
Ptolemy: they declared him king
of Cilicia, of Syria, of Phoenicia.
Caesarion was standing well in front,
attired in rose-colored silk,
on his chest a garland of hyacinths,
his belt a double row of sapphires and amethysts,
his shoes laced up with white
ribbons embroidered with pink-skinned pearls.
Him they declared greater than the boys:
him they declared King of Kings.

The Alexandrians were certainly aware
that these were merely words, a bit of theatre.

* * *

But the day was warm and poetic, the sky pale blue,
the Alexandrian Gymnasium
a triumphant artistic achievement,
the courtiers' elegance exceptional,
Caesarion all grace and beauty
(Cleopatra's son, of Lagid blood):
and the Alexandrians rushed to the festival,
filled with excitement, and shouted acclaim
in Greek, and in Egyptian, and some in Hebrew,
enchanted by the lovely spectacle –
though of course they knew what they were worth,
what empty words these kingdoms were.

PHILHELLENE

Take care the engraving's artistically done.
Expression grave and majestic.
The diadem better rather narrow;
I don't care for those wide ones, the Parthian kind.
The inscription, as usual, in Greek:
nothing excessive, nothing grandiose –
the proconsul mustn't get the wrong idea,
he sniffs out everything and reports it back to Rome –
but of course it should still do me credit.
Something really choice on the other side:
some lovely discus-thrower lad.
Above all, I urge you, see to it
(Sithaspes, by the god, don't let them forget)
that after the "King" and the "Savior"
the engraving should read, in elegant letters,
        "Philhellene."
Now don't start in on me with your quips,
your "Where are the Greeks?" and "What's Greek
here, behind the Zágros, beyond Phráata?"
Many, many others, more oriental than ourselves,
write it, and so we'll write it too.
And after all, don't forget that now and then
sophists come to us from Syria,
and versifiers, and other devotees of puffery.
Hence unhellenised we are not, I rather think.

[*1906*; 1912]   35

THE STEPS

On an ebony bed that is adorned
with eagles made of coral, Nero sleeps
deeply – heedless, calm, and happy;
flush in the prime of the flesh,
and in the beautiful vigor of youth.

But in the alabaster hall that holds
the ancient shrine of the Ahenobarbi
how uneasy his Lares are!
The little household gods are trembling,
trying to hide their slight bodies.
For they've heard a ghastly sound,
a fatal sound mounting the stairs,
footsteps of iron that rattle the steps.
And, faint with fear now, the pathetic Lares,
wriggle their way to the back of the shrine;
each jostles the other and stumbles
each little god falls over the other
because they've understood what kind of sound it is,
have come to know by now the Erinyes' footsteps.

THE TOMB OF LYSIAS THE GRAMMARIAN

Just there, on the right as you go in,
in the Beirut library we buried him:
the scholar Lysias, a grammarian.
The location suits him beautifully.
We put him near the things that he
remembers maybe even there – glosses, texts,
apparatuses, variants, the multivolume works
of scholarship on Greek idiom. Also, like this,
his tomb will be seen and honored by us
as we pass by on our way to the books.

[*1911*; 1914]

TOMB OF EURION

Inside of this elaborate memorial,
made entirely of syenite stone,
which so many violets, so many lilies adorn,
Eurion lies buried, so beautiful.
A boy of twenty-five, an Alexandrian.
Through the father's kin, old Macedonian;
a line of alabarchs on his mother's side.
With Aristoclitus he took his philosophical instruction;
rhetoric with Parus. A student in Thebes, he read
the sacred writings. He wrote a history
of the Arsinoïte district. This at least will endure.
Nevertheless we've lost what was most dear: his beauty,
which was like an Apollonian vision.

DANGEROUS

Said Myrtias (a Syrian student
in Alexandria; during the reign
of the *augustus* Constans and the *augustus* Constantius;
partly pagan, and partly Christianized):
"Strengthened by contemplation and study,
I will not fear my passions like a coward.
My body I will give to pleasures,
to diversions that I've dreamed of,
to the most daring erotic desires,
to the lustful impulses of my blood, without
any fear at all, for whenever I will –
and I will have the will, strengthened
as I'll be by contemplation and study –
at the crucial moments I'll recover
my spirit as it was before: ascetic."

[?; 1911]

MANUEL COMNENUS

The emperor Lord Manuel Comnenus
one melancholy morning in September
sensed that death was near. The court astrologers
(those who were paid) were nattering on
that he had many years yet left to live.
But while they went on talking, the king
recalls neglected habits of piety,
and from the monastery cells he orders
ecclesiastical vestments to be brought,
and he puts them on, and is delighted
to present the decorous mien of a priest or friar.

Happy are all who believe,
and who, like the emperor Lord Manuel, expire
outfitted most decorously in their faith.

IN THE CHURCH

I love the church – its labara,
the silver of its vessels, its candelabra,
the lights, its icons, its lectern.

When I enter there, inside of a Greek Church:
with the aromas of its incenses,
the liturgical chanting and harmonies,
the magnificent appearance of the priests,
and the rhythm of their every movement –
resplendent in their ornate vestments –
my thoughts turn to the great glories of our race,
to our Byzantium, illustrious.

[*1892*; *1901*; *1906*; 1912?]

VERY RARELY

He's an old man. Worn out and stooped,
crippled by years, and by excess,
stepping slowly, he moves along the alleyway.
But when he goes inside his house to hide
his pitiful state, and his old age, he considers
the share that he – *he* – still has in youth.

Youths recite his verses now.
His visions pass before their animated eyes.
Their healthy, sensuous minds,
their well-limned, solid flesh,
stir to his own expression of the beautiful.

IN STOCK

He wrapped them up carefully, neatly
in green silken cloth, very costly.

Roses from rubies, pearls into lilies,
amethyst violets. Lovely the way that *he* sees,

and judges, and wanted them; not in the way
he saw them in nature, or studied them. He'll put
    them away,

in the safe: a sample of his daring, skillful work.
Whenever a customer comes into the store,

he takes other jewels from the cases to sell –
    fabulous things –
bracelets, chains, necklaces, rings.

PAINTED

To my craft I am attentive, and I love it.
But today I'm discouraged by the slow pace of
    the work.
My mood depends upon the day. It looks
increasingly dark. Constantly windy and raining.
What I long for is to see, and not to speak.
In this painting, now, I'm gazing at
a lovely boy who's lain down near a spring;
it could be that he's worn himself out from running.
What a lovely boy; what a divine afternoon
has caught him and put him to sleep. –
Like this, for some time, I sit and gaze.
And once again, in art, I recover from creating it.

MORNING SEA

Here let me stop. Let me too look at Nature for a while.
The morning sea and cloudless sky
a brilliant blue, the yellow shore; all
beautiful and grand in the light.

Here let me stop. Let me fool myself: that these are
        what I see
(I really saw them for a moment when I first stopped)
instead of seeing, even here, my fantasies,
my recollections, the ikons of pleasure.

[?; 1916]

SONG OF IONIA

Because we smashed their statues all to pieces,
because we chased them from their temples –
this hardly means the gods have died.
O land of Ionia, they love you still,
it's you whom their souls remember still.
And as an August morning's light breaks over you
your atmosphere grows vivid with their living.
And occasionally an ethereal ephebe's form,
indeterminate, stepping swiftly,
makes its way along your crested hills.

IN THE ENTRANCE OF THE CAFÉ

Something they were saying close to me
drew my attention to the entrance of the café.
And I saw the lovely body that looked as if
Eros had made it using all his vast experience:
crafting with pleasure his shapely limbs;
making tall the sculpted build;
crafting the face with emotion
and leaving behind, with the touch of his hands,
a feeling in the brow, the eyes, and the lips.

[*1904?*; >1915]

ONE NIGHT

The room was cheap and tawdry,
hidden above that suspect restaurant.
From the window you could see the alley,
filthy and narrow. From below
came the voices of some working men
who were playing cards and having a good time.

And there, in that common, vulgar bed
I had the body of love, I had the lips,
sensuous and rose-colored, of drunkenness –
the rose of such a drunkenness, that even now
as I write, after so many years have passed!,
in my solitary house, I am drunk again.

COME BACK

Come back often and take hold of me,
beloved feeling come back and take hold of me –
when the memory of the body reawakens,
and old longing once more passes through the blood;
when the lips and skin remember,
and the hands feel like they're touching once again.

Come back often and take hold of me at night,
when the lips and skin remember ...

[*1904; 1909;* 1912]

HE SWEARS

Now and then he swears   to begin a better life.
But when the night comes on   with its own ideas,
its own compromises,   and with its promises:
but when the night comes on   with a power of its own,
of a body that desires and demands, he returns,
lost, once more to the same fateful pleasure.

I WENT

No restraint. I surrendered completely and I went.
To gratifications that were partly real,
partly careening within my mind –
I went in the illuminated night.
And I drank powerful wines, just as
the champions of pleasure drink.

[*1905*; *1913*]

CHANDELIER

In a small and empty room, four lone walls,
covered in a cloth of solid green,
a beautiful chandelier burns and glows
and in each and every flame there blazes
a wanton fever, a wanton need.

In the small room, which has been set
aglow by the chandelier's powerful flames,
the light that appears is no ordinary light.
The pleasure of this heat has not been fashioned
for bodies that too easily take fright.

SINCE NINE –

Half past twelve. The time has quickly passed
since nine o'clock when I first turned up the lamp
and sat down here. I've been sitting without reading,
without speaking. With whom should I speak,
so utterly alone within this house?

The apparition of my body in its youth,
since nine o'clock when I first turned up the lamp,
has come and found me and reminded me
of shuttered perfumed rooms
and of pleasure spent – what wanton pleasure!
And it also brought before my eyes
streets made unrecognizable by time,
bustling city centres that are no more
and theatres and cafés that existed long ago.

The apparition of my body in its youth
came and also brought me cause for pain:
deaths in the family; separations;
the feelings of my loved ones, the feelings of
those long dead which I so little valued.

Half past twelve. How the hours have passed.
Half past twelve. How the years have passed.

[1917; 1918]   55

COMPREHENSION

The years of my youth, my pleasure-bent existence –
how plainly do I see their meaning now.

What useless, foolish regrets . . .

But I didn't see their meaning then.

In the dissolute life I led in my youth
my poetry's designs took shape;
the boundaries of my art were drawn.

That is why the regrets were never firm.
And my resolutions – to master myself, to change –
would last for two weeks at the most.

CAESARION

In part to ascertain a certain date
and in part to while away the time,
last night I took down a collection
of Ptolemaic inscriptions to read.
The unstinting laudations and flatteries
are the same for all. All of them are brilliant,
glorious, mighty, beneficent;
every undertaking utterly wise.
As for the women of the line, they too,
all the Berenices and the Cleopatras, are wonderful.

When I successfully ascertained the date
I'd have finished with the book, if a tiny,
insignificant reference to King Caesarion
hadn't attracted my attention suddenly......

Ah, there: you came with your vague
charm. In history there are only a few
lines that can be found concerning you;
and so I could fashion you more freely in my mind.
I fashioned you this way: beautiful and feeling.
My artistry gives to your face
a beauty that has a dreamy winsomeness.
And so fully did I imagine you
that yesterday, late at night, when the lamp

went out – I deliberately let it go out –
I dared to think you came into my room,
it seemed to me you stood before me: as you must
    have been
in Alexandria after it had been conquered,
pale and wearied, perfect in your sorrow,
still hoping they'd have mercy on you,
those vile men – who whispered "too many Caesars."

NERO'S DEADLINE

Nero wasn't worried when he heard
the prophecy of the Delphic Oracle.
"Let him beware the age of seventy-three."
He still had time to enjoy himself.
He is thirty years old. It's quite sufficient,
this deadline that the god is giving him,
for him to think about dangers yet to come.

Now to Rome he'll be returning a little wearied,
but exquisitely wearied by this trip
which had been endless days of diversion –
in the theatres, in the gardens, the gymnasia. . . .
Evenings of the cities of Achaea . . .
Ah, the pleasure of naked bodies above all . . .

So Nero. And in Spain, Galba
was secretly assembling his army and preparing it:
the old man, seventy-three years old.

[*1915*; 1918]

ONE OF THEIR GODS

Whenever one of Them would cross Seleucia's
marketplace, around the time that evening falls –
like some tall and flawlessly beautiful boy,
with the joy of incorruptibility in his eye,
with that dark and fragrant hair of his –
the passersby would stare at him
and one would ask another if he knew him,
and if he were a Syrian Greek, or foreign. But some,
who'd paid him more attention as they watched,
understood, and would make way.
And as he disappeared beneath the arcades,
among the shadows and the evening lights,
making his way to the neighborhood that comes alive
only at night – that life of revels and debauch,
of every known intoxication and lust –
they'd wonder which of Them he really was
and for which of his suspect diversions
he'd come down to walk Seleucia's streets
from his Venerable, Sacrosanct Abode.

TOMB OF LANES

The Lanes whom you loved isn't here, Marcus,
in the tomb where you come and cry, and stay for hours
        and hours.
The Lanes whom you loved you have much closer
        to you,
at home, when you shut yourself in and look at his
        picture:
it preserves some part of what was precious in him,
it preserves some part of what you had loved.

Remember, Marcus, how you brought the famed
Cyrenian painter back from the proconsul's palace,
and with what artful cunning he attempted
to persuade you both, no sooner had he seen your friend,
that he simply *had* to do him as Hyacinth
(which would make his portrait so much better known).

But your Lanes didn't loan out his beauty like that;
and objecting firmly he told him to represent
neither Hyacinth nor anybody else,
but Lanes, son of Rhametichos, an Alexandrian.

[*1916*; 1918]

TOMB OF IASES

Here I lie: Iases. Throughout this great city I was
     renowned
for being the most beautiful boy.
Admired by men of deep learning – and also by the
     less profound,
the common folk. Both gave equal joy

to me. But they took me so often for a Narcissus or
     a Hermes
that excess wore me out, and killed me. Passerby,
if you're an Alexandrian you won't judge me.
     You know the yearnings
of our life; what heat they hold; what pleasures
     most high.

IN A CITY OF OSRHOENE

From the tavern brawl they brought him back to us,
    wounded –
our friend Rhemon, around midnight yesterday.
Through the windows we'd left open all the way
the moon illumined his beautiful body on the bed.
We're a hodgepodge here: Syrians, Greeks,
    Armenians, Medes.
Rhemon too is such a one. But yesterday, as the moon
shone its light upon his sensuous face
we were put in mind of Plato's Charmides.

[*1916*; 1917]

TOMB OF IGNATIUS

Here I'm not the Cleon who's renowned
in Alexandria (where they aren't easily impressed)
for my fabulous houses, for my gardens,
for my horses and my chariots,
for the diamonds and the silks I wore.
Far from it: here I'm not that Cleon.
May those twenty-eight years be erased.
I am Ignatius, a Lector, who very late
came to my senses. But still I lived ten blessed months
in the serenity and security of Christ.

64   [*1916*; 1917]

IN THE MONTH OF HATHOR

With difficulty I read   upon this ancient stone
"O Lo[r]d Jesus Christ."   I can just discern a "So[u]l."
"In the mon[th] of Hathor"   "Leuciu[s] went to his re[s]t."
Where they record his age   "The span of years he li[ve]d"
the Kappa Zeta is proof   that he went to his rest a youth.

Amidst the erosion I see   "Hi[m] ... Alexandrian."
Then there are three lines   radically cut short;
but some words I can make out —   like "our t[e]ars,"
                                                    "the pain,"
"tears" again further down,   and "grief for [u]s,
                                                    his [f]riends."
In love, it seems to me,   Leucius was greatly blessed.
In the month of Hathor   Leucius went to his rest.

[*1917*; 1917]   65

FOR AMMON, WHO DIED AT
29 YEARS OF AGE, IN 610

Raphael, they want you to compose
some verses as an epitaph for the poet Ammon.
Something very artistic and polished. You'll be able,
you're the perfect choice, to write what's suitable
for the poet Ammon, one of our own.

Certainly you'll talk about his poetry –
but do say something, too, about his beauty,
about the delicate beauty that we loved.

Your Greek is always beautiful and musical.
But now we want all of your craftsmanship.
Into a foreign tongue our pain and love are passing.
Pour your Egyptian feeling into a foreign tongue.

Raphael, your verses should be written
so that they have, you know, something of our lives
        within them,
so that the rhythm and every phrasing makes it clear
that an Alexandrian is writing of an Alexandrian.

WHENEVER THEY ARE AROUSED

Try to keep watch over them, poet,
although few of them can be restrained:
Your eroticism's visions.
Place them, partly hidden, in your phrases.
Try to keep hold of them, poet,
whenever they're aroused within your mind,
at night or in the brightness of midday.

[*1913*; 1916]

TO PLEASURE

Joy and balm of my life the memory of the hours
when I found and held on to pleasure as I wanted it.
Joy and balm of my life – for me, who had no use
for any routine enjoyment of desire.

I HAVE GAZED SO MUCH –

At beauty I have gazed so much
that my vision is filled with it.

The body's lines. Red lips. Limbs made for pleasure.
Hair like something taken from Greek statues:
always lovely, even when it's uncombed,
and falls, a bit, upon the gleaming brow.
Faces of love, exactly as
my poetry wanted it ... in the nights of my youth,
secretly encountered in my nights ....

[*1911*; 1917]   69

IN THE STREET

His appealing face, somewhat pallid;
his chestnut eyes, looking tired;
twenty-five years old, but looks more like twenty;
with something artistic about his clothes
– something in the color of the tie, the collar's shape –
aimlessly he ambles down the street,
as if still hypnotized by the illicit pleasure,
by the very illicit pleasure he has had.

THE WINDOW OF THE TOBACCO SHOP

Nearby the illuminated window
of a tobacco shop they stood, in the midst of
    many others.
Quite by chance their glances happened to meet,
and timorously, hesitantly expressed
the illicit longing of their flesh.
Later, on the pavement, a few nervous steps –
until they smiled, and nodded very faintly.

And afterward the closed carriage....
the sensitive nearing of their bodies;
the hands as one, the lips as one.

[*1907*; 1917]   71

PASSAGE

What he timidly imagined in his school days, is
    opened up,
revealed to him. And he makes the rounds, stays out
    all night,
gets swept up in things. And as is (for our art)
    only right,
pleasure rejoices in his fresh, hot blood,
an outlaw sensual abandon overcomes
his body; and his youthful limbs
give in to it.
               And so a simple boy
becomes, for us, worth looking at, and passes through
    the High
World of Poetry, for a moment – yes, even he;
this aesthete of a boy, with his blood so fresh and hot.

IN EVENING

At any rate it wouldn't have lasted long. Years
of experience make that clear to me. But still, Fate
came and ended things in too much of a hurry.
The life of loveliness was brief.
But how powerful our perfumed unctions were,
how exquisite the bed in which we lay,
to what pleasure we gave our bodies away.

A reverberation of the days of pleasure,
a reverberation of those days drew near me,
something we two had in youth, the fire;
once more I took a letter in my hands,
and read it over and over, till the light failed.

And I went out onto the balcony, melancholy –
went out so I might clear my head by seeing at least
a little of this town I love so well,
some little movement in the street, and in the shops.

[*1916*; 1917]

GRAY

Looking at an opal of medium gray,
I remembered two beautiful gray eyes
that I saw; it must be twenty years ago....

....

For one month we were in love.
Then the departure, for Smyrna I daresay,
to get work there, and we never saw each other again.

Those gray eyes – if they're alive – will have
        grown ugly;
the beautiful face will have fallen into ruins.

O my memory, keep them as they were.
And, memory, whatever you can bring back from that
        love of mine,
whatever you can, bring back to me tonight.

BELOW THE HOUSE

Yesterday while strolling through a neighborhood
on the edge of town, I passed below the house
I used to go in when I was very young.
There Eros had taken possession of my body
with his exquisite force.

                  And yesterday
as I passed along that ancient street,
suddenly everything was made beautiful by
     desire's spell:
the shops, the pavements, the stones,
and walls, and balconies, and windows;
there was nothing ugly that remained.

And while I was standing, gazing at the door,
and standing, tarrying by the house,
the foundation of all my being yielded up
the sensual emotion that was stored inside.

[*1917*; 1919]

THE NEXT TABLE

Can't be more than twenty-two years old.
And yet I'm sure that, just about the same
number of years ago, I enjoyed that very body.

It's not at all a flaring of desire.
And I only came to the casino a little while ago;
I haven't even had time to drink a lot.
This very body: I enjoyed it.

And if I don't remember where – one slip doesn't signify.

Ah there, sitting at the next table now:
I recognize each movement – and beneath the clothes
I see once more the naked limbs I loved.

76   [*1918*; 1919?]

REMEMBER, BODY

Body, remember not just how much you were loved,
not just the beds where you have lain,
but also those longings that so openly
glistened for you in the eyes,
and trembled in the voice – and some
chance obstacle arose and thwarted them.
Now that it's all finally in the past
it almost seems as if you gave yourself to
those longings, too – remember how
they glistened, in the eyes that looked at you;
how they trembled in the voice, for you;
      remember, body.

[*1916*; 1917/1918]

From

POEMS 1919–1932

THE AFTERNOON SUN

This room, how well I know it.
Now they're renting it out, with the one next door,
as commercial offices. The whole house has become
offices for middlemen, and businessmen, and Companies.

Ah, this room, how familiar it is.

Near the door, here, was the sofa,
and in front of it a Turkish rug;
Close by, the shelf with two yellow vases.
On the right – no, opposite, a dresser with a mirror.
In the middle, the table where he'd write;
and the three big wicker chairs.
Near the window was the bed
where we made love so many times.

They must be somewhere still, poor things.

Near the window was the bed:
the afternoon sun came halfway up.

... At four o'clock in the afternoon, we'd parted
for one week only ... Alas,
that week became an eternity.

[*1918*; 1919]   81

TO STAY

One in the morning it must have been,
or half past one.
                    In a corner of that dive;
in back of the wooden partition.
Apart from the two of us, the place completely empty.
A kerosene lamp barely shed some light.
The waiter who'd been sitting up was sleeping by
        the door.

No one would have seen us. But
we were so on fire for each other
that caution was beyond us anyway.

Our clothes were half undone – we weren't wearing
        much,
since it was blazing hot, a heavenly July.

Delight in flesh amidst
clothes half undone:
quick baring of flesh – the image of it
has crossed twenty-six years; and now has come
to stay here in this poetry.

82   [*1918*; 1919]

OF THE JEWS (50 A.D.)

Painter and poet, runner and thrower,
Endymion's beauty: Ianthes, son of Antonius.
From a family close to the Synagogue.

"The days that I most value are the ones
when I abandon the aesthetic quest,
when I forsake the beauty and rigor of the Hellenic,
with its overriding preoccupation
with perfectly formed and perishable white limbs.
And I become what I would like
always to remain: of the Jews, of the holy Jews,
        the son."

A bit too heated, this declaration of his. "Always
remain of the Jews, of the holy Jews —"

But he didn't remain one at all.
The Hedonism and Art of Alexandria
made the boy into their devotee.

[*1912*; <1919?>]   83

ABOARD THE SHIP

It certainly resembles him, this small
pencil likeness of him.

Quickly done, on the deck of the ship:
an enchanting afternoon.
The Ionian Sea all around us.

It resembles him. Still, I remember him as handsomer.
To the point of illness: that's how sensitive he was,
and it illumined his expression.
Handsomer, he seems to me,
now that my soul recalls him, out of Time.

Out of Time. All these things, they're very old –
the sketch, and the ship, and the afternoon.

YOUNG MEN OF SIDON (400 A.D.)

The actor whom they'd brought to entertain them
declaimed, as well, a few choice epigrams.

The salon opened onto the garden;
and had a delicate fragrance of blooms
that was mingled together with the perfumes
of the five sweetly scented Sidonian youths.

Meleager, and Crinagoras, and Rhianus were read.
But when the actor had declaimed
"Here lies Euphorion's son, Aeschylus, an Athenian –"
(stressing, perhaps, more than was necessary
the "valour far-renowned," the "Marathonian lea"),
at once a spirited boy sprang up,
mad for literature, and cried out:

"Oh, I don't like that quatrain, not at all.
Expressions like that somehow seem like cowardice.
Give – so I proclaim – all your strength to your work,
all your care, and remember your work once more
in times of trial, or when your hour finally comes.
That's what I expect from you, and what I demand.
And don't dismiss completely from your mind
the brilliant Discourse of Tragedy –
that Agamemnon, that marvelous Prometheus,

those portrayals of Orestes and Cassandra,
that *Seven Against Thebes* – and leave, as your memorial,
only that you, among the ranks of soldiers,
        the masses –
that you too battled Datis and Artaphernes."

THAT THEY COME –

One candle is enough.   Its faint light
is more fitting,   will be more winsome
when come Love's –   when its Shadows come.

One candle is enough.   Tonight the room
can't have too much light.   In reverie complete,
and in suggestion's power,   and with that little light –
in that reverie: thus   will I dream a vision
that there come Love's –   that its Shadows come.

[?; 1920]

DARIUS

The poet Phernazes is working on
the crucial portion of his epic poem:
the part about how the kingdom of the Persians
was seized by Darius, son of Hystaspes. (Our
glorious king is descended from him:
Mithridates, Dionysus and Eupator.) But here
one needs philosophy; one must explicate
the feelings that Darius must have had:
arrogance and intoxication, perhaps; but no – more
like an awareness of the vanity of grandeur.
Profoundly, the poet ponders the matter.

But he's interrupted by his servant, who comes
running and delivers the momentous intelligence:
The war with the Romans has begun.
Most of our army has crossed the border.

The poet stays, dumbfounded. What a disaster!
How, now, can our glorious king,
Mithridates, Dionysus and Eupator,
be bothered to pay attention to Greek poems?
In the middle of a war – imagine, Greek poems.

Phernazes frets. What bad luck is his!
Just when he was sure, with his "Darius,"

to make his name, and to reduce his critics,
those envious men, to silence at long last.
What a setback, what a setback for his plans!

And if it's only a setback: fine.
But let's see if we're really all that safe
in Amisus. It's not a spectacularly well-fortified town.
The Romans are most fearsome enemies.
Is there any way we can get the best of them,
we Cappadocians? Could it ever happen?
Can we measure up to the legions now?
Great gods, protectors of Asia, help us. –

And yet in the midst of all his upset, and the disaster,
a poetic notion stubbornly comes and goes –
far more convincing, surely, are arrogance and
        intoxication;
arrogance and intoxication are what Darius would
        have felt.

[*<1897?; 1917; 1920*]   89

THEIR BEGINNING

The fulfillment of their illicit pleasure
is accomplished. They've risen from the bed,
and dress themselves quickly without speaking.
They emerge separately, secretly, from the house.
   And while
they walk rather uneasily in the street, it seems
as if they suspect that something about them betrays
what kind of bed they'd lain in just before.

Nonetheless, how the artist's life has gained.
Tomorrow, the day after, or through the years
   he'll write
powerful lines that had their beginning here.

MELANCHOLY OF JASON,
SON OF CLEANDER:
POET IN COMMAGENE: 595 A.D.

The aging of my body and my looks
is a wound from a terrible knife.
I have no means whatsoever to endure it.
To you I turn, Art of Poetry,
you who know something of drugs;
of attempts to numb pain, in Imagination and Word.

It's a wound from a terrible knife. –
Bring on your drugs, Art of Poetry,
which make it impossible – for a while – to feel
    the wound.

[*1918?*; *1921*]

I BROUGHT TO ART

I'm sitting and musing.   I brought to Art
longings and feelings –   some half-glimpsed
faces or lines;   some uncertain mem'ries
of unfulfilled loves.   Let me submit to it.
It knows how to shape   the Form of Loveliness;
almost imperceptibly   filling out life,
piecing together impressions,   piecing together the days.

FROM THE SCHOOL OF THE
RENOWNED PHILOSOPHER

He remained Ammonius Saccas's student for two years;
but of philosophy and of Saccas he grew bored.

Afterward he went into politics.
But he gave it up. The Prefect was a fool;
and those around him solemn, pompous stiffs;
their Greek horribly uncouth, the wretches.

His curiosity was aroused,
a bit, by the Church: to be baptized,
to pass as a Christian. But he quickly
changed his mind. He'd surely get in a row
with his parents, so ostentatiously pagan:
and they'd immediately put an end – an awful thought –
to his extremely generous allowance.

Still, he had to do something. He became an habitué
of the depraved houses of Alexandria,
of every secret den of debauchery.

In this, fortune had been kind to him:
had given him a form of highest comeliness.
And he delighted in that heavenly gift.

For at least another ten years yet
his beauty would endure. After that –
perhaps to Saccas he would go once more.
And if in the meantime the old man died,
he'd go to some other philosopher or sophist;
someone suitable can always be found.

Or in the end, it was possible he'd even return
to politics – admirably mindful
of his family traditions,
duty to one's country, and other pomposities of that sort.

THOSE WHO FOUGHT ON BEHALF OF
THE ACHAEAN LEAGUE

You brave, who fought and fell in glory:
who had no fear of those who'd conquered everywhere.
You blameless, even if Diaeus and Critolaus blundered.
Whensoever the Greeks should want to boast,
"Such are the men our race produces" is what they'll say
about you. That's how marvelous the praise for you
     will be. –

Written in Alexandria by an Achaean:
in the seventh year of Ptolemy, the "Chickpea."

[*1922; 1922*]

IN AN OLD BOOK

In an old book – about a hundred years old –
I found, neglected among the leaves,
a watercolour without a signature.
It must have been the work of a very powerful artist.
It bore the title "Representation of Love."

But "– of the love of extreme sensualists" would have
  been more fitting.

For it was clear as you looked at this work
(the artist's idea was easily grasped)
that the youth in this portrait wasn't meant
for those who love in a somewhat wholesome way,
within the limits of what is strictly permitted –
with his chestnut-brown, intensely colored eyes;
with the superior beauty of his face,
the beauty of unusual allures;
with those flawless lips of his that bring
pleasure to the body that it cherishes;
with those flawless limbs of his, made for beds
called shameless by the commonplace morality.

IN DESPAIR

He's lost him utterly.   And from now on he seeks
in the lips of every new   lover that he takes
the lips of that one: his.   Coupling with every new
lover that he takes   he longs to be mistaken:
that it's the same young man,   that he's giving himself
                                                    to *him*.

He's lost him utterly,   as if he'd never been.
The other wished – he said –   he wished to save himself
from that stigmatized   pleasure, so unwholesome;
from that stigmatized   pleasure, in its shame.
There was still time, he said –   time to save himself.

He's lost him utterly,   as if he'd never been.
In his imagination,   in his hallucinations
in the lips of other youths   he seeks the lips of that one;
He wishes that he might   feel his love again.

THEATRE OF SIDON (400 A.D.)

A respectable citizen's son —   above all else, a beauteous
youth who belongs to the theatre,   agreeable in so
                                                                  many ways:
I now and then compose,   in the language of the Greeks,
exceedingly daring verses,   which I circulate
very secretly, of course —   gods! they mustn't be seen
by those who prate about morals,   those who wear
                                                                  gray clothes —
verses about a pleasure   that is select, that moves
toward a barren love   of which the world disapproves.

BEFORE TIME COULD ALTER THEM

They were very pained   when they parted company.
They themselves didn't want it;   it was just the way
                                                          things were.
The need to make a living   was forcing one of them
to go far away –   New York or Canada.
Certainly their love   wasn't the same as before;
the attraction had been   gradually diminished,
its attraction had been   very much diminished.
But still, that they should part –   that they didn't want.
It was just the way things were. –   Or perhaps it was
                                                          that Fate
was something of an artist,   separating them now
before their feeling died away,   before Time could
                                                          alter them:
Each one, for the other,   will be as if he'd stayed
twenty-four years old,   the exquisite lad.

[*1924?*; 1924]

HE CAME TO READ –

He came so he might read. Lying open
are two or three books: historians and poets.
But he'd barely read for ten minutes,
when he put them aside. On the sofa
he's half asleep. He's completely devoted to books –
but he's twenty-three years old, and very handsome;
and this afternoon desire has come
to his flawless flesh, and to his lips.
To his flesh, which is beauty entire,
the fever of desire has come;
without foolish shame about the form of its
    enjoyment. . . .

OF COLORED GLASS

One detail in particular greatly moves me
about the crowning, in Blachernae, of John Cantacuzenus
and Irene, Andronicus Asen's daughter.
As they had very little in the way of precious stones
(our wretched dominion's poverty was great)
they wore artificial ones. A heap of bits of glass,
scarlet, green, or blue. There was nothing
that was abject or unsuitable
in my eyes about those little pieces
of colored glass. On the contrary, they look
like a piteous protestation against
the unjust misfortune of those who were being crowned.
They are the symbols of what was fitting for them
    to have,
of what above all it was right for them to have
at their crowning: for a Lord John Cantacuzenus,
for a Lady Irene, Andronicus Asen's daughter.

[1925]

THE 25TH YEAR OF HIS LIFE

He frequently goes into the tavern
where they'd met each other the month before.
He asked; but there was nothing they could tell him.
From what they said, he understood he'd met
someone who was totally unknown;
one of the many unknown and suspicious
youthful types who were often passing through.
Still, he goes to the tavern frequently, at night,
and sits and looks toward the entrance;
he grows weary looking toward the entrance.
Perhaps he'll come in. Tonight, perhaps he'll come.

For close to three weeks this is what he does.
His mind has grown sick with wantonness.
On his mouth the kisses have remained.
All his flesh is suffering from the constant yearning.
The feel of the other's body is upon him.
He wants to be as one with it again.

Not to give himself away: this is what he tries for,
　　　of course.
But sometimes he's almost indifferent. –
Besides, he knows what he's exposing himself to,
he's made up his mind. It's not unlikely that the life
　　　he's living
will lead him to some devastating scandal.

102　[*1918?*; *1925*]

ON THE ITALIAN SEASHORE

Cemus, son of Menedorus,   a young Italiote,
passes through his life   immersed in his amusements:
this is what they're used to,   the youths of
                                        Greater Greece,
who have been brought up   with enormous wealth.

But today he is extremely   (contrary to his nature)
broody and dejected.   Close to the seashore,
in deepest melancholy,   he sees that they're unloading
the vessels with the plunder   from the Peloponnese.

Spoils of the Greeks: the pillage from Corinth.

O surely it is not   permissible today,
it isn't possible for   the young Italiote
to have any desire   at all for his amusements.

[1925]

IN THE BORING VILLAGE

In the boring village where he works –
an employee in a general
store; extremely young – and where he's waiting
for another two or three months to pass,
for another two or three months till business tapers off,
so he can make for the city and throw himself
straight into its bustle and amusements:
in the boring village where he's waiting –
he fell into his bed this evening sick with desire,
all his youth inflamed with carnal yearning,
with beautiful intensity, all his beautiful youth.
And pleasure came into his sleep; within
his sleep he sees and possesses the shape, the flesh
he wanted....

CLEITUS'S ILLNESS

Cleitus, an extremely amiable
boy of twenty-three or thereabouts –
with the best of educations, with a rare Greek culture –
is gravely ill. The fever has got him,
the one that's swept through Alexandria this year.

The fever also found him morally wracked,
anguished because his friend, a certain young actor,
has ceased loving him and wanting him.

He's gravely ill, and his parents are terrified.

And a certain old housemaid who raised him
is also full of fear for Cleitus's life.
In her terrible anxiety
she is put in mind of an idol
she once worshipped as a girl, before she came here
      as a maid
to the home of distinguished Christians, and herself
      became a Christian.
She secretly takes some cakes, and wine, and honey.
She brings them before the idol. She chants as many
litanies as she recalls: the bits from either end, the
      middles. The foolish woman
doesn't realize that it matters little to the black demon
whether a Christian is or isn't cured.

[1926]   105

IN A MUNICIPALITY OF ASIA MINOR

The tidings of the outcome of the naval battle, at Actium,
were rather unexpected, to be sure.
But there's no need to draft a new inscription.
The name alone need change. Instead of (there,
in the final lines) "Having saved the Romans
from that calamitous Octavian,
a man who's like a parody of Caesar,"
now we'll put "Having saved the Romans
from that calamitous Marc Antony."
The entire text fits beautifully.

"To the conqueror, the most glorious,
unsurpassed in every martial action,
astounding for his political achievements,
on behalf of whom the people fervently prayed
for the triumph of Marc Antony"
here, as we said, the switch: "of Caesar,
considering him the finest gift of Zeus –
to the powerful protector of the Greeks,
who benevolently reverences all Greek customs,
is beloved in every region that is Greek,
so richly worthy of encomia,
and of the narration of his deeds at length
in the Greek tongue, both in verse and prose:
in the Greek tongue, which is the bearer of renown,"
etcetera, etcetera. It all fits brilliantly.

106   [1926]

PRIEST OF THE SERAPEUM

The good old man my father
the one who always loved me just the same,
the good old man my father I now mourn,
who died two days ago, a bit before the break of day.

O Jesus Christ, that I might observe
the commandments of your most holy church
in every deed of mine, in every word,
in every thought, is my endeavor
every day. And from those who deny you
I turn my face. – But now I mourn:
I lament, O Christ, for my father
for all that he was – dreadful to utter it –
a priest at the accursed Serapeum.

[1926]

IN THE TAVERNS

In the public houses   and in the lowest dives
of Beirut I wallow.   I didn't want to stay
in Alexandria: not I.   Tamides has left me;
he went off with the Eparch's   son so he could get
a villa on the Nile,   a palace in the city.
It wouldn't do for me   to stay in Alexandria. –
In the public houses   and the lowest dives
of Beirut I wallow.   In low debauchery
I spend my sordid hours.   The only thing that saves me,
like a lasting beauty,   like a perfume that
has lingered on my flesh,   is that, for two years,
Tamides was all mine,   the most exquisite youth,
all mine – not for a house,   nor a villa on the Nile.

SOPHIST DEPARTING FROM SYRIA

Learned sophist, you   who are quitting Syria
and have in mind to write   about Antioch,
it's fitting that you mention   Mebes in your work.
Mebes the renowned,   who's undeniably
the most beauteous youth,   the one who's most beloved,
in all of Antioch.   No one of the other
youths who lead that life –   none of them is paid
as highly as he is.   In order to have Mebes
for two or three days only,   they very often give him
up to a hundred staters. –   I said, In Antioch:
but also in Alexandria,   but also even in Rome,
you cannot find a youth   as desirable as Mebes.

[1926]

JULIAN AND THE ANTIOCHENES

*The Chi, so they say, in no wise harmed the city, nor did the
Kappa ... Finding ourselves interpreters ... we learned that
letters were the initials of names, and that the former meant
Christ, and the latter, Constantius.*

JULIAN, *Misopogon*

Was it ever possible for them to give up
their beautiful way of life; the rich array
of their daily entertainments; their glorious
theatre where was born a union of Art
and the erotic predilections of the flesh!

Immoral to a point – quite likely to a great extent –
that they were. But they had the satisfaction that their
    way of life
was the *much discussed* life of Antioch,
pleasure-bent, absolutely elegant.

To give up all of that, and turn to *what*, precisely?

His airy prattle concerning the false gods,
his wearisome braggadocio;
his childish fear of the theatre;
his graceless prudishness; his ridiculous beard.

O certainly they preferred the Chi,
O certainly they preferred the Kappa; a hundred
    times more.

DAYS OF 1896

He debased himself completely.   An erotic inclination,
very much forbidden   and held in great contempt
(innate, all the same)   was the reason why:
the society he lived in   was extremely priggish.
He had gradually lost   what little money he had;
afterwards his position,   then his reputation.
He was nearing thirty   and had never held
a job for even a year,   at least that anyone knew of.
Sometimes he would meet   his expenses by
playing go-between   in deals considered shameful.
He ended up the sort   who, if you were seen with him
often, you'd likely be   extremely compromised.

But that's not all of it;   that wouldn't be fair.
The memory of his beauty   deserves a great deal more.
There's another way of looking   and, if seen that way,
he strikes you as attractive;   strikes you as the
                                        simple, true
child of desire   who, above his honor
and his reputation,   placed, without a thought,
the unsullied pleasure   of his unsullied body.

Above his reputation?   But society, which was
so extremely priggish   had such foolish values.

[*1925*; 1927]   111

TWO YOUNG MEN, 23 TO 24 YEARS OLD

Since half past ten he'd waited at the café,
expecting him to appear before too long.
Midnight came and went – and still he waited.
Half past one had come and gone: the café
had emptied out entirely, almost.
He grew bored of reading the newspapers
mechanically. Of his three poor shillings
only one was left: during his long wait
he'd squandered all the rest on coffee and cognac.
He smoked all the cigarettes he had.
All the waiting was exhausting him. Because,
alone as he had been for many hours, he
began to be possessed by irksome thoughts
about the wayward life that he was living.

But when he saw his friend come in – all at once
the weariness, the boredom, the thoughts all fled.

His friend brought some unexpected news:
In the card game he'd won sixty pounds.

Their handsome faces, their exquisite youth,
the sensitive love that they shared between them,
was refreshed, revived, invigorated by
the sixty pounds from the game of cards.

All joy and potency, feeling and beauty,
they went – not to the houses of their upstanding
    families
(where, at any rate, they were no longer wanted):
to a certain one they knew, and rather special,
to a house of vice they went, and asked for
a bedroom, and expensive drinks, and they drank again.

And when the expensive drinks had all been drained,
and when it was close to four o'clock in the morning,
happy, they gave themselves to love.

[1927]   113

DAYS OF 1901

This was the thing about him that stood out:
that even with all of his loose living,
and such a vast experience of the sensual;
for all that it was usually the case
that his attitude was so well-fitted to his age,
there would be moments – to be sure,
extremely rare – when the impression that
he gave was one of flesh almost untouched.

The beauty of his nine-and-twenty years,
which had been assayed so much by pleasure,
reminded one at moments, strangely enough,
of a lad who – somewhat awkwardly – for
the first time gives his pure body up to love.

A YOUNG MAN, SKILLED IN THE ART
OF THE WORD – IN HIS 24TH YEAR

Keep working however you can, brain. –
A one-sided passion is wasting him away.
He is in a maddening situation.
He kisses the beloved face each day,
his hands upon those most exquisite limbs.
Never before has he loved with such great
passion. But what's missing is the beautiful fulfillment
of love; what's missing is the fulfillment
which both of them must long for with the same
       intensity.

(They're not equally devoted to abnormal pleasure;
       not both of them.
He alone is utterly possessed by it.)

And he wastes away, his nerves completely shot.
Besides, he's out of work; that makes things worse.
With a bit of trouble he borrows some
small sums of money (which he practically
has to beg for, sometimes) and barely gets by.
He kisses the lips he worships: he takes his pleasure
upon the exquisite body – which, however,
he now feels is merely acquiescing.
And then he drinks and smokes; he drinks and smokes;

and drags himself around the cafés all day long,
wearily drags the wasting of his beauty. –
Keep working however you can, brain.

PORTRAIT OF A YOUNG MAN OF
TWENTY-THREE DONE BY HIS FRIEND
OF THE SAME AGE, AN AMATEUR

He finished up the portrait   yesterday at noon. Now
he studies it in detail.   He did him in a gray
jacket, all unbuttoned,   a deep gray. Without
any vest or tie.   In a shirt of rose;
so a little of   the beauty of the chest,
the beauty of the throat,   might show through a bit.

The right side of his brow   is almost totally
covered by his hair,   by his beautiful hair
(which is combed the way   he fancies it this year).
The note is utterly   the voluptuous one
that he wanted to strike   when he did the eyes,
when he did the lips ...   That mouth of his, the lips
made for the fulfillment   of a choice eroticism.

[1928]

POTENTATE FROM WESTERN LIBYA

Overall he was well liked in Alexandria,
during the ten days that he sojourned there,
Aristomenes, the son of Menelaus,
the potentate from Western Libya.
Like his name, his attire, too, quite suitably, was Greek.
He gratefully received his honors, although
he didn't court them; he was unpretentious.
He'd spend his time shopping for Greek books,
history and philosophy especially.
Above all, however: a person of few words.
He must have been a deep thinker, it was widely said,
and for such men it's only natural not to talk too much.

No deep thinker was he; no anything.
A commonplace, laughable sort of person.
He took a Greek name, dressed like the Greeks,
learned, more or less, to behave like the Greeks;
and in his heart he dreaded that by some chance
he'd lose the goodish impression that he'd made
by speaking a terribly barbaric Greek
and that the Alexandrians would poke fun at him,
as is their wont, horrid people.

For this reason he confined himself to a few words,
frightfully attentive to his declensions and his accent;
and grew bored to death, with all those
conversations piled up inside him.

118   [1928]

DAYS OF 1909, '10, AND '11

He was the son of a much put-upon, impoverished
sailor (from an island in the Aegean Sea).
He worked at a blacksmith's. He wore threadbare
      clothes;
his workshoes split apart, the wretched things.
His hands were completely grimed with rust and oil.

Evenings, when he was closing up the shop,
if there was anything he was really longing for,
some tie that cost a little bit of money,
some tie that was just right for a Sunday,
or if in a shop window he'd seen and yearned for
some beautiful shirt in mauve:
one or two shillings is what he'd sell his body for.

I ask myself whether in antique times
glorious Alexandria possessed a youth more beauteous,
a lad more perfect than he – for all that he was lost:
for of course there never was a statue or portrait of him;
thrown into a blacksmith's poor old shop,
he was quickly spoiled by the arduous work,
the common debauchery, so ruinous.

MYRES: ALEXANDRIA IN 340 A.D.

When I learned the dreadful news, that Myres was dead,
I went to his house, for all that I am loath
to go inside the homes of Christians,
above all those in mourning, or on feast-days.

I stood there in a corridor. I didn't want
to go in any further, since I perceived
that the kinsmen of the dead man were looking at me
with evident dismay, and with displeasure.

They had him in a large room
a part of which I saw from where I stood
off to the side: all expensive carpets,
and services of silver and of gold.

I stood crying on one side of the corridor.
And I was thinking that our gatherings and outings
wouldn't be worth much, without Myres, from now on;
and was thinking that I'd no longer see him
at our splendid and outrageous all-night revels,
enjoying himself, and laughing, and declaiming lines
with that perfect feel he had for Greek rhythm;
and was thinking that I'd lost forever more
his beauty, that I'd lost forever more
the youth whom I once worshipped to distraction.

120

Some old women, near me, were speaking softly
about the last day that he was alive –
the name of Christ always on his lips,
a cross that he was holding in his hands. –
Later on there came into the room
four Christian priests, and they fervently
recited prayers and orisons to Jesus,
or to Mary (I don't know their religion very well).

We knew, of course, that Myres was a Christian.
From the very first we knew it, when
two years ago he joined our little band.
But he lived his life completely as we did.
Of all of us, the most devoted to his pleasures;
squandering lavish sums on his amusements.
Blithely untroubled by what people thought,
he threw himself eagerly into street brawls late at night,
whenever our gang chanced upon a rival gang.
Never once did he speak about his religion.
In fact, there was one time when we told him
that we were taking him with us to the Serapeum.
But he seemed to be unhappy with
this little joke of ours: I remember now.
Ah, and two other times now come to mind.
When we were making libations to Poseidon,

he pulled out of our circle, and turned his gaze
        elsewhere.
When one of us, in his enthusiasm,
said, May our company ever be under
the favor and protection of the great,
the all-beautiful Apollo – Myres murmured
(the others didn't hear) "except for me."

Their voices raised, the Christian priests
were praying for the soul of the young man. –
I stood observing with how much diligence,
and with what intense attention
to the protocols of their religion, they were preparing
everything for the Christian funeral rite.
And all of a sudden I was seized by a queer
impression. Vaguely, I had the feeling that
Myres was going far away from me;
had a feeling that he, a Christian, was being united
with his own, and that I was becoming
a stranger to him, very much a stranger; I sensed besides
a certain doubt coming over me: perhaps I had been
        fooled
by my passion, had always been a stranger to him. –
I flew out of their horrible house,
and quickly left before their Christianity
could get hold of, could alter, the memory of Myres.

BEAUTIFUL, WHITE FLOWERS AS THEY WENT SO WELL

He went into the café   where they used to go together.
Here his friend had said   just three months ago:
"We haven't got a cent.   We two are so poor
that we've come to this –   the cheapest spots in town.
I'll put it to you straight: I can't keep going out
with you. Someone else –   *listen* – wants me now."
That someone else had promised   him two suits and some
silken handkerchiefs. –   To get him back again
his friend made quite a fuss,   and came up with
                                    twenty pounds.
He came back to him   for the twenty pounds.
But not just only that: for their old affection,
and for their old love,   and for their old feelings.
That "someone" was a liar,   a real low character.
He'd had only one   suit made for him and
that, begrudgingly: he had to plead a thousand times.

But he no longer wants   any suits at all
nor indeed wants any   silken handkerchiefs,
neither twenty pounds,   not even twenty pence.

They buried him on Sunday,   at ten o'clock in the
                                    morning.
They buried him on Sunday: scarcely a week ago.

123

On his shabby coffin   he laid some flowers,
beautiful, white flowers   as they went so well
with his beauty and   his two-and-twenty years.

When at night he went —   he happened to have some
                                        business,
something absolutely vital —   into the café where they
used to go together: a dagger in his heart,
that dismal black café,   where they used to go together.

COME NOW, KING OF THE LACEDAEMONIANS

Cratesicleia did not condescend to let
the people see her crying and lamenting;
magnificent she went about, and silent.
Never did her imperturbable mien reveal
her dejection or her torment.
But even so, for a moment she could not hold back:
and before she went aboard the ship to go to
    Alexandria,
she took her son to the temple of Poseidon,
and when they found themselves alone she clasped
    him to her bosom
and kept kissing her son, who was "tormented," says
Plutarch, "and in a state of very great distress."
Still, her strong character prevailed:
pulling herself together, the remarkable woman
said to Cleomenes "Come now, O king
of the Lacedaemonians, and when we go forth
from here, let no one see us weeping
nor doing anything that is unworthy of
Sparta. This alone is ours to do;
our fortunes go howsoever the god provides."

And onto the ship she went, making her way to
    that "provides."

IN THE SAME SPACE

House, coffeehouses, neighborhood: setting
that I see and where I walk; year after year.

I crafted you amid joy and amid sorrows:
out of so much that happened, out of so many things.

And you've been wholly *remade into feeling*; for me.

THE MIRROR IN THE ENTRANCE

In the entrance hallway of that sumptuous home
there was an enormous mirror, very old;
acquired at least eighty years ago.

A strikingly beautiful boy, a tailor's assistant,
(on Sunday afternoons, an amateur athlete),
was standing with a package. He handed it
to one of the household, who then went back inside
to fetch a receipt. The tailor's assistant
remained alone, and waited.
He drew near the mirror, and stood gazing at himself,
and straightening his tie. Five minutes later
they brought him the receipt. He took it and left.

But the ancient mirror, which had seen and seen again,
throughout its lifetime of so many years,
thousands of objects and faces –
but the ancient mirror now became elated,
inflated with pride, because it had received upon itself
perfect beauty, for a few minutes.

[1930]   127

HE ASKED ABOUT THE QUALITY –

From within the office where he'd been taken on
to fill an insignificant, ill-paid position
(eight pounds a month at best: bonuses included)
he emerged, when he'd finished the solitary task
at which he'd been stooped the entire afternoon.
He left at seven, and then strolled slowly along,
and dawdled in the street. – Handsome;
interesting, too: in a way that showed he'd realized
a maximal yield from his senses.
He'd just turned twenty-nine, the month before.

He dawdled in the street, and in the shabby
alleyways that led to where he lived.

As he passed before a little store
where the goods that were for sale were
shoddy, low-priced things for laborers,
he saw a face within, he saw a shape;
they urged him on and he went in, as if keen
on seeing colored handkerchiefs.

He asked about the quality of the handkerchiefs,
and what they cost; in a voice that was choked,
almost stifled by his yearning.
So, too, the answers that came back:

distracted, in a voice kept very low,
secretly concealing consent.

Now and then they'd talk about the merchandise – but
their sole aim: for their hands to touch
atop the handkerchiefs; for their faces to
draw near, and their lips, as if by chance.
Some momentary contact of their limbs.

Quickly and secretly, so the proprietor
wouldn't notice, sitting there in back.

[1930]

ACCORDING TO THE FORMULAS OF
ANCIENT GRECO-SYRIAN MAGICIANS

"What distillation is there to be found, from magic
herbs," an aesthete said,
"what distillation, made according to the formulas
of ancient Greco-Syrian magicians,
that could, for one day (if its power can't
last more than that), or just a little while,
bring me back the age of twenty-three
again; bring my friend at twenty-two years old
back to me again – his beauty, and his love.

"What distillation is there to be found, made according
        to the formulas
of ancient Greco-Syrian magicians
that, in keeping with this movement back in time,
might even bring us back our little room once more."

DAYS OF 1908

That year he found himself without a job;
and so he made a living from cards,
from backgammon, and what he borrowed.

A job, at three pounds a month, at a little stationer's,
had been offered to him.
But he turned it down without the slightest hesitation.
It wouldn't do. It wasn't a wage
for him, a young man with some education,
      twenty-five years of age.

Two or three shillings a day was what he'd get,
      sometimes not.
What could the boy possibly earn from cards and
      backgammon
in the coffeehouses of his class, the common ones,
however cleverly he played, however stupid the
      partners he chose?
And loans – then there were those loans.
It was rare that he'd manage a crown, more often it
      was half;
sometimes he'd settle for shillings.

Sometimes for a week, occasionally more,
when he was spared the horror of staying up till dawn,

he'd cool off at the baths, with a swim at morning.

His clothes were in a dreadful state.
There was one suit that he would always wear,
a suit of a very faded cinnamon hue.

Oh days of the summer of nineteen-hundred eight,
your vision, quite exquisitely, was spared
that very faded cinnamon-colored suit.

Your vision preserved him
as he was when he undressed, when he flung off
the unworthy clothes, and the mended underwear.
And he'd be left completely nude; flawlessly beautiful;
    a thing of wonder.
His hair uncombed, springing back;
his limbs a little colored by the sun
from his nakedness in the morning at the baths, and at
    the seashore.

From
THE SENGOPOULOS
NOTEBOOK
(1897–1908)

VOICES

Imagined voices, and beloved, too,
of those who died, or of those who are
lost unto us like the dead.

Sometimes in our dreams they speak to us;
sometimes in its thought the mind will hear them.

And with their sound for a moment there return
sounds from the first poetry of our life –
like music, in the night, far off, that fades away.

[*1894*; 1894; *1903*; 1904]   135

LONGINGS

Like the beautiful bodies of the dead who never aged,
shut away inside a splendid tomb by tearful mourners
with roses at their head and jasmine at their feet –
that's what longings look like when they've passed away
without being fulfilled, before they could be made
          complete
by just one of pleasure's nights, or one of its
          shimmering mornings.

CANDLES

The days of the future stand before us
like a row of little lighted candles –
golden, warm, and vibrant little candles.

The days that have gone by remain behind us,
a melancholy line of candles now snuffed out;
the closest still give off their smoke,
cold candles, melted down, bent out of shape.

I don't want to see them; their appearance saddens me,
and I'm saddened, too, to recall their former light.
I look in front of me, at my lighted candles.

I don't want to turn around lest I see and tremble at
how quickly the darkened line is growing longer,
how quickly the snuffed-out candles multiply.

[*1893*; 1899]   137

AN OLD MAN

In the noisy café, right in the middle,
an old man sits bent over the table;
his newspaper in front of him, with no one for company.

And in his contempt for his wretched old age,
he thinks how very little he enjoyed
the years when he had strength, and wit, and beauty.

He knows he's aged a lot: he feels it, sees it.
And even so, the moment when he was young seems
like yesterday. How brief a span, how brief a span.

And he brooded on the way that Prudence had
      duped him:
and how he'd always trusted – so stupidly! –
the lie she told: "Tomorrow. You have lots of time."

He remembers the impulses he bridled; and how
much joy he sacrificed. His foolish caution, now,
is mocked by each lost opportunity.

... But all this thinking, all this remembering
makes the old man dizzy. And leaning
on the table in the café, he falls asleep.

138   [*1894*; 1897]

PRAYER

The sea took into her depths a sailor's life. —
Unaware, his mother goes and lights

a taper before the image of Our Lady
that the weather might be fair, and his return speedy —

while at the wind she always strains her ears.
But as she prays the ikon hears,

solemn and full of mourning,
knowing that the son she waits for won't be returning.

[*1896*; 1898]   139

OLD MEN'S SOULS

Inside their old bodies, so wasted away,
the souls of old men sit around.
How woebegone the poor things are, and
how bored by the wretched life they live.
How afraid they are of losing it and how they love it,
these bewildered and contradictory
souls, which sit around – tragicomic –
inside their old hides, so worn away.

THE FIRST STEP

To Theocritus one day the young
poet Eumenes was complaining:
"By now two years have passed since I've been writing
and I've only done a single idyll so far.
It's the only work that I've completed.
O woe is me, I see how high it is,
Poetry's stairway; very high indeed.
And from where I stand, on this first step,
I shall never ascend. Unhappy me!"
Theocritus replied: "The words you speak
are unbecoming; they are blasphemies.
Even if you're on the first step, you ought
to be dignified and happy.
To have got this far is no small thing;
what you have done is a glorious honor.
Even that first step, even the first,
is very far removed from the common lot.
In order for you to proceed upon this stair
you must claim your right to be
a citizen of the city of ideas.
It is difficult, and rare as well,
to be entered into that city's rolls.
In its agora you'll find Legislators
whom no mere adventurer can fool.
To have got this far is no small thing;
what you have done is a glorious honor."

[*1895*; 1899]   141

INTERRUPTION

It's we who interrupt the work of the immortals,
we hasty, inexperienced creatures of a moment.
In the palaces of Eleusis and of Phthia
Demeter and Thetis initiate good works
amidst high flames and dense smoke.
But Metaneira always comes rushing in from the
royal halls, her hair disheveled, terrified,
and Peleus always takes fright, and interferes.

THERMOPYLAE

Honor to all of those who in their lives
have settled on, and guard, a Thermopylae.
Never stirring from their obligations;
just and equitable in all of their affairs,
but full of pity, nonetheless, and of compassion;
generous whenever they're rich, and again
when they're poor, generous in small things,
and helping out, again, as much as they are able;
always speaking nothing but the truth,
yet without any hatred for those who lie.

And more honor still is due to them
when they foresee (and many do foresee)
that Ephialtes will make his appearance in the end,
and that the Medes will eventually break through.

[1901; 1903]

CHE FECE ... IL GRAN RIFIUTO

For certain people there comes a day
when they are called upon to say the great Yes
or the great No. It's clear at once who has
the Yes within him at the ready, which he will say

as he advances in honor, in greater self-belief.
He who refuses has no second thoughts. Asked
again, he would repeat the No. And nonetheless
that No – so right – defeats him all his life.

THE WINDOWS

In these shadowed rooms, in which I pass
gloomy days, up and down I pace
that I might find the windows. – For a window
to be open would be a consolation. –
But there are no windows, or I can't
find them. And perhaps it's best I don't.
Perhaps the light will be a new oppression.
Who knows what new things it will show.

[*1897*; *1903*]

WALLS

Without pity, without shame, without consideration
they've built around me enormous, towering walls.

And I sit here now in growing desperation.
This fate consumes my mind, I think of nothing else:

because I had so many things to do out there.
O while they built the walls, why did I not look out?

But no noise, no sound from the builders did I hear.
Imperceptibly they shut me off from the world without.

WAITING FOR THE BARBARIANS

– What is it that we are waiting for, gathered in
  the square?

  The barbarians are supposed to arrive today.

– Why is there such great idleness inside the
  Senate house?
Why are the Senators sitting there, not passing
  any laws?

  Because the barbarians will arrive today.
  Why should the Senators still be making laws?
  The barbarians, when they come, will legislate.

– Why is it that our Emperor awoke so early today,
  and has taken his position at the greatest of the
   city's gates
seated on his throne, in solemn state, wearing
  the crown?

  Because the barbarians will arrive today.
  And the emperor is waiting to receive
  their leader. Indeed he is prepared
  to present him with a parchment scroll. In it
  he's conferred on him many titles and honorifics.

– Why is it that our consuls and our praetors come
        outside today
    wearing their scarlet togas with their rich embroidery,
    why have they donned their armlets with all their
        amethysts,
    and rings with their magnificent, glistening emeralds;
    why should they be carrying such precious staves
        today,
    maces chased exquisitely with silver and with gold?

    Because the barbarians will arrive today;
    and things like that bedazzle the barbarians.

– Why do our worthy orators not come today as usual
    to deliver their addresses, each to say his piece?

    Because the barbarians will arrive today;
    and they're bored by eloquence and public speaking.

– Why is it that such uneasiness has seized us all at once,
    and such confusion? (How serious the faces have
        become.)
    Why is it that the streets and squares are emptying
        so quickly,
    and everyone's returning home in such deep
        contemplation?

Because night has fallen and the barbarians
    haven't come.
And some people have arrived from the borderlands,
and said there are no barbarians anymore.

And now what's to become of us without barbarians.
Those people were a solution of a sort.

[*1898*; 1904]

From

REPUDIATED POEMS
(1886–1898)

BUILDERS

Progress is a giant edifice – each hefts
his stone: one words, counsels, another
deeds – and every day it lifts its head
higher. Should some tempest, some sudden

storm approach, the good builders make haste
all as one to shield their wasted labor.
Wasted, because the life of each is passed
embracing ills and sorrows for a future generation,

that this generation might know an artless
happiness, and length of days, and wealth, and wisdom
without base sweat, or servile industry.

But it will never live, this fabled generation;
its very perfection will cast this labor down
and once again their futile toil will begin.

[1891]

BARD

Far from the world, poetic magic makes him drunk;
　　　　all the world, for him, is lovely verse.
For her bard, Imagination built a house: strong,
　　　　incorporeal, which fortune will not jar.

You will say: "A cold and futile life. Foolishness
　　　　to think that life's the pleasurable sounds
of a flute and nothing else" or "Hard-heartedness
　　　　afflicts the man who's never been worn down

by the pain of life's travail." And yet your judgment
　　　　is error and injustice. His nature is god-sent.
Judge not in your reasoned, blind affliction.

The walls of his house are magic emerald –
　　　　and in them voices whisper: "Friend, be tranquil:
reflect and sing. Take heart, mystic apostle!"

TIMOLAUS THE SYRACUSAN

Timolaus is the premier musician
of the premier city in all of Sicily.
Throughout this Western Greece of ours the Greeks
from Neapolis, and from Massalia,
from Tarentum, from Panormus, and Akragas,
and from any other cities of Hesperia
whose shores are crowned with Hellenism,
converge en masse in Syracuse
to attend the concerts of the famed musician.
Preëminent in the lyre and the kithara,
he is skilled as well upon the piffero,
the tenderest of tender flutes. He draws
from the douçaine a plangent melody.
And when he takes the psalterium in his hands
its chords bring forth the poetry
of sultry Asia – an initiation
into voluptuous and dulcet reverie,
fragrance of Ecbatana and Ninus.

. . . .

. . . .

But amidst the many accolades,
amid the gifts of many talents' worth,
the goodly Timolaus is utterly wretched.
Ruddy Samian does not hearten him,
and by his silence he insults the symposium.

An indefinable grief takes hold of him,
grief for his great insufficiency.
He senses that his instruments are empty,
even as his soul is filled with music.
Painfully, persistently he struggles
to find an outlet for the mystic sounds.
His most perfect harmonies remain
silent and concealed inside of him.
The crowd in its enthusiasm marvels at
the very things he censures and contemns.
The clamorous sound of accolades disturbs him,
and amid the gifts of many talents' worth
distractedly he stands there, the musician.

SWEET VOICES

Those voices are the sweeter which have fallen
      forever silent, mournfully
resounding only in the heart that sorrows.

In dreams the melancholic voices come,
      timorous and humble,
and bring before our feeble memory

the precious dead, whom the cold cold earth
      conceals; for whom the mirthful
daybreak never shines, nor springtimes blossom.

Melodious voices sigh; and in the soul
      our life's first poetry
sounds – like music, in the night, that's far away.

[1894]

HOURS OF MELANCHOLY

The happy sully Nature.
The earth's a realm of grief.
The dawn weeps tears of unknown woe.
The orphaned evenings, pallid, grieve.
And the soul that is elect sings mournfully.

In breezes I hear sighing.
In violets I see blame.
I feel the rose's painful life;
the meadows filled with cryptic woe.
And in the woodland thick a sobbing sounds.

Mankind lauds the happy.
And poets false extol them.
But Nature's gates are closed to those
who, heartless and indifferent, laugh,
laugh: strangers in a miserable land.

OEDIPUS

The Sphinx has fallen on him
with teeth and claws unsheathed
and with all her nature's savagery.
At her first onslaught Oedipus fell down,
terrified, at first, by her appearance –
until now he'd never have imagined
a countenance like this, such speech as this.
But though the monster ramps with both her feet
upon the breast of Oedipus,
he recovered swiftly – nor does he in the least
fear her now, since he has
the answer ready and will vanquish her.
And yet he takes no pleasure in this victory.
His eye, with melancholy filled,
does not behold the Sphinx, but sees beyond
the narrow road that goes to Thebes
and will come to its conclusion at Colonus.
And in his soul there is a clear foreboding
that there the Sphinx will speak to him again
with much more difficult and with far greater
riddles for which there isn't any answer.

[1896]

NEAR AN OPEN WINDOW

In the stillness of an autumn night,
I sit near an open window,
for entire hours, in a perfect,
voluptuous tranquility.
The gentle rainfall of the leaves descends.

The keening of the perishable world
resounds within my perishable nature,
but is a dulcet keening, rising like a prayer.
My window opens up an unknown
world. A fount of fragrant memories,
unutterable, appears before me.
Against my window wings
are beating – chill autumnal exhalations
approach me and encircle me
and in their holy tongue they speak to me.

I feel vague and wide-embracing
hopes; and in the hallowed silence
of creation, my ears hear melodies,
hear the crystalline, the mystic
music of the chorus of the stars.

160   [1896]

HORACE IN ATHENS

In the bedchamber of the hetaera Leah,
where all is style and wealth, a downy bed,
a youth, with jasmine on his hands, is speaking.
His fingers are adorned with many gems,

and he wears a snow-white silk himation
picked out in scarlet, in the eastern fashion.
His speech is Attic of the purest strain
but a gentle stress in his pronunciation

betrays a trace of Tiber and of Latium.
The young man is avowing his adoration,
and silently she listens, the Athenian,

to her lover Horace, so mellifluent;
and stupefied, she sees new worlds of Beauty
within the passion of the great Italian.

[1897]

THE TARENTINES HAVE THEIR FUN

Theatres filled, music everywhere;
here debauch and lechery, and there
contests for athletes and philosophers.
Dionysus's statue is embellished with a crown
unwithering. No corner of the land remains unstrewn
with offerings. The people of Tarentum have their fun.

But the Senators withdraw from all of these
and glowering say many angry things.
And each barbarian toga as it leaves
seems to be a storm-cloud, threatening.

162   [1898]

From

UNPUBLISHED
POEMS
(1877?–1923)

TO STEPHANOS SKILITSIS

If souls, as they tell us, are immortal,
perhaps your spirit wanders near us, Stephanos,
and feels contentment when you hear your name
upon our lips, and when our faithful thoughts
are stirred by your beloved memory.

Stephanos, you've not been parted from us by the grave:
from us, with whom you nearly shared your life.
As children we would play together; our childish woes
and our joys we'd feel together; and then, young men,
we discovered life's first pleasures all as one –
till two days ago, Stephanos, two days ago, and now
we have borne you, cold, to your last abode.

But no. You're with us. The stone upon your grave
will be, for us, a delicate veil, diaphanous.
And though you're lost to your friends' eyes, their souls,
and memories, and hearts, will always see you
and keep you, Stephanos, their inseparable friend.

"NOUS N'OSONS PLUS CHANTER
LES ROSES"

Fearing what is commonplace,
I stifle many of my words.
In my heart are written many
poems; and I love the lays
that are there interred.

O first, pure, only liberty
of youth, penchant for pleasure!
O sweet drunkenness of senses!
I fear lest base banality
your forms divine dishonour.

THE HEREAFTER

I believe in the Hereafter. Material appetites
or love for the real don't beguile me. It's not habit
but instinct. The heavenly word will be added

to life's imperfect sentence, otherwise inane.
Respite and reward will follow upon action.
When sight is closed forevermore to Creation,

the eye will be opened in the presence of the Creator.
An immortal wave of life will flow from each and every
Gospel of Christ – wave of life uninterrupted.

[1892]

IN THE CEMETERY

When to the cemetery memory
directs your steps,
worship the sacred mystery
of our darkling future, devoutly.
Lift up your mind to the Lord.
Before you
the most narrow bed of slumbers infinite
lies beneath the pity of Jesus.

Our beloved religion hallows our memorials,
hallows our death.
For the pagans' gifts and ceremonials
and sacrifices she has no love.
Without any foolish offerings
of gold,
the most narrow bed of slumbers infinite
lies beneath the pity of Jesus.

EPITAPH

Stranger, by the Ganges here I lie, a man
who lived a life of lamentation, toil, and pain;
a Samian, I ended in this thrice-barbaric land.
This grave close by the riverside contains

many woes. Undiluted lust for gold
drove me into this accursed trade.
I was shipwrecked on the Indian coast and sold
as a slave. Well into old age

I wore myself out, worked until I breathed no more –
deprived of Greek voices, and far from the shore
of Samos. What I suffer now is not, therefore,

fearful; and I voyage down to Hades without grief.
There among compatriots I shall be.
And forever after I shall speak in Greek.

[1893]

DREAD

At night, O Christ my Lord,
protect for me my soul and my mind
when about me there begin to roam
Beings and Things that have no name
and they run with fleshless feet around my room
and make a circle round my bed that they might see me –
and gaze upon me as though they know me
cackling voicelessly because they've frightened me.

I know it, yes, they lie in wait for me
as though they were mulling over the foul times
when perhaps I crept along with them – in the murk,
entangled with those beings and with those things.
And they're frenzied to think those times will
come again.
But they won't come again; for I am saved,
in the name of Christ I've been baptized.

I tremble when at night I sense,
when I feel that there in the dense
gloom their eyes are staring down at me....
Hide me from their sight, my Lord.
And when they speak or croak, do not allow
any of their blasphemies to reach my ears,
lest it happen that they bring to my soul
some dreadful reminder of the hidden things they know.

170   [1894]

IN THE HOUSE OF THE SOUL

Deeper, at the deepest part in the House of the Soul,
Where they come and go and sit around a fire,
The Passions with their women's faces.

RODENBACH

In the House of the Soul the Passions wander –
    beautiful women gowned
in silks, and sapphires crown their heads.
From the door of the house to its innermost depths
                        they command
all of the chambers. Within the grandest –
    on nights when their blood is inflamed –
they dance and they drink with their hair unbound.

Outside the chambers, pale and poorly dressed
    in a bygone era's garments,
the Virtues wander and in bitterness listen
to the merrymaking of their drunken companions.
To the glass of the windows they press their faces
    and, contemplative, they watch in silence
the lights, the jewels, and the blossoms of the dance.

JULIAN AT THE MYSTERIES

But when he found himself amid the darkness,
amid the terrifying depths of the earth,
in the company of godless Greeks,
and saw the disembodied forms emerge before him
with apparitions, and with brilliant lights,
for a moment he was afraid, this youth,
and an instinct from his pious years
returned, and he made the sign of the cross.
Immediately the Forms disappeared.
The visions were gone – the lights went out.
The Greeks sneaked glances at each other.
And the young man said: "Did you see that marvel?
My dear companions, I am afraid.
I am afraid, my friends, I want to go.
Did not you see the spirits straightaway
vanish at the moment when I made
the blessed shape of the cross?"
There was much guffawing from the Greeks.
"For shame, for shame that you should speak such words
to us, who are philosophers and sophists.
If you like, go tell such things to the man
of Nicomedia, and tell them to his priests.
Before you there appeared the greatest gods
of our illustrious Greece.
And if they left, do not think for a minute

that they were frightened by a gesture.
It's merely that when they saw you make
that extremely base and boorish shape
their noble nature was repelled,
and they left and held you in contempt."
This is what they said, and from his fear,
which was holy and blessed,
the foolish man recovered, and was persuaded
by the godless words of the Greeks.

[*1896*]

IMPOSSIBLE THINGS

There is one joy alone, but one that's blessed,
one consolation only in this pain.
How many thronging vulgar days were missed
because of this ending; how much ennui.

A poet has said: "The loveliest
music is the one that cannot be played."
And I, I daresay that by far the best
life is the one that cannot be lived.

GARLANDS

Absinthe, datura, and hypoceme,
aconite, hellebore, and hemlock –
all of the bitter and poisonous –
give up their leaves and their terrible flowers
that they might become the great garlands
that are placed on the radiant altar –
ah, the shining altar of Malachite stone –
of the Passion both dreadful and sublime.

[1897]

ADDITION

Whether I am happy or unhappy, I don't calculate.
But one thing always I joyfully keep in sight –
that in the great addition (the addition of those I hate)
that comprises such great numbers, I don't count
as one of the many units there. I wasn't numbered in
    the great
addition. And for me that delight is sufficient.

STRENGTHENING

Whoever longs to make his spirit stronger
should leave behind respect and obedience.
Some of the laws are ones that he will keep,
but for the most part he will contravene
both laws and ethics, and he will leave behind
the norms that are received, inadequate.
Many things will he be taught by pleasures.
He will never fear the destructive act;
half the house must be demolished.
Thus will he grow virtuously into knowledge.

SEPTEMBER OF 1903

At least let me be fooled by delusions, now;
so I might not feel my empty life.

And I was so close so many times.
And how I froze, and how I was afraid;
why should I remain with lips shut tight;
while within me weeps my empty life,
and my longings wear their mourning black.

To be, so many times, so close
to the eyes, and to the sensual lips,
to the dreamed of, the beloved body.
To be, so many times, so close.

DECEMBER 1903

Even though I may not speak about my love –
I may not talk about your hair, or your lips,
    or your eyes;
still, your face, which I keep inside my soul;
the sound of your voice, which I keep inside my mind;
the September days that dawn within my dreams:
my words and phrases take their shape and color
    from these,
whatever subject I may touch upon, whatever idea
    I may be speaking of.

[1904]

JANUARY OF 1904

Ah this January, this January's nights,
when I sit and refashion in my thoughts
those moments and I come upon you,
and I hear our final words, and hear the first.

This January's despairing nights,
when the vision goes and leaves me all alone.
How swiftly it departs and melts away –
the trees go, the streets go, the houses go, the lights go:
it fades and disappears, your erotic shape.

ON THE STAIRS

As I was going down the shameful stair,
you came in the door, and for a moment
I saw your unfamiliar face and you saw me.
Then I hid so you wouldn't see me again, and you
passed by quickly as you hid your face,
and stole inside the shameful house
where you likely found no pleasure, just as I found none.

And yet the love you wanted, I had to give you;
the love I wanted – your eyes told me so,
tired and suspicious – you had to give me.
Our bodies sensed and sought each other out;
our blood and skin understood.

But we hid from each other, we two, terrified.

[1904]   181

IN THE THEATRE

I grew bored with looking at the stage,
and raised my eyes to the loge.
And there inside a box I saw you
with your queer beauty, and your spoilt youth.
And straightaway there came back to my mind
all they'd told me about you, that afternoon,
and my thoughts and my body were stirred.
And whilst I gazed enchanted
at your weary beauty, at your weary youth,
at your discriminating attire,
I imagined you and I depicted you,
in just the way they'd talked about you, that afternoon.

POSEIDONIANS

. . . like the Poseidonians in the Tyrrhenian Gulf whom it befell
that, although of Greek origin, they became utterly barbarized,
becoming Tyrrhenians or Romans, and changing their lan-
guage along with many of their customs. Yet to this day they
observe a certain Greek holiday, during which they gather
together and recall the ancient names and customs; after which,
lamenting loudly to each other and weeping, they depart.

ATHENAEUS

The Greek language the Poseidonians
had forgotten after centuries of intermingling
with Tyrrhenians and Latins, and other foreigners.
The one ancestral feature they retained
was a Greek festival, with elaborate rites,
with lyres and oboes, with contests and garlands.
It was their custom, at the festival's conclusion,
to tell each other of their ancient practices
and to pronounce Greek words again,
which but a few of them any longer understood.
And their holiday would always end in melancholy.
For they'd remember then that they too were Greeks –
they too Italiotes, once upon a time.
And now how far they'd fallen, what had they become
that they should live and speak like barbarians,
removed – disastrous fate! – from the culture of
     the Greeks.

[1906]

HIDDEN

From all I did and from all I said
they shouldn't try to find out who I was.
An obstacle was there and it distorted
my actions and the way I lived my life.
An obstacle was there and it stopped me
on many occasions when I was going to speak.
The most unnoticed of my actions
and the most covert of all my writings:
from these alone will they come to know me.
But perhaps it's not worth squandering
so much care and trouble on puzzling me out.
Afterwards – in some more perfect society –
someone else who's fashioned like me
will surely appear and be free to do as he pleases.

HEARING OF LOVE

On hearing of a powerful love tremble and be moved
like an aesthete. But then, contented,
remember how many your imagination fashioned
        for you: those
first: and then the others – lesser – that in your
        life you've
experienced and enjoyed, those more real,
        and tangible. –
You were not deprived of loves like these.

THAT'S HOW

In this obscene photograph, which is secretly
sold in the street (so the police won't see),
in this smutty photograph
how could there be a face like this,
of dreams; how could you be here.

Who knows what degraded, sordid life you lead;
how horrid the surroundings must have been
when you posed so they could photograph you;
what a tawdry soul yours must be.
But given all of this, and more, to me you remain
the face that comes in dreams, a figure
fashioned for and dedicated to Greek pleasure –
that's how you are for me still and how my poetry
      speaks of you.

186   [*1913*]

THEOPHILUS PALAEOLOGUS

The final year is this one. The final Greek
emperor is this one. And alas
what dismal things they're saying all around him.
In his desperation, in his pain
the Lord Theophilus Palaeologus
says "I'd rather die than live."

Ah, Lord Theophilus Palaeologus,
how much of the yearning of our race, how much of
    its exhaustion
(how much weariness from injustice and persecution)
those five tragic words of yours contained.

[*1914*]

AND I GOT DOWN AND I LAY THERE
IN THEIR BEDS

When I went inside the house of pleasure
I didn't linger in the parlor where they celebrate
conventional desires, with some decorum.

The rooms I went to were the secret ones
and I got down and I lay there in their beds.

The rooms I went to were the secret ones,
the ones they think it shameful even to name.
But for me there was no shame – for if there were
what kind of poet, what kind of craftsman would I be?
Better to abstain completely. That would be more
       in keeping,
much more in keeping with my poetry
than going to the common parlor for my pleasure.

SIMEON

I know them, yes, those new poems of his.
All Beirut is passionate about them.
I'll take a careful look at them another day.
Today I can't, since I'm quite upset.

Certainly he's better versed in Greek than Libanius.
But even better than Meleager? I don't believe so.

Ah, Mebes, so what of Libanius! and so what of books!
and all such trivialities! ..... Mebes, yesterday I was –
quite by chance it happened – at the foot of
    Simeon's pillar.

I slipped in among the Christians
who were praying silently and worshipping,
and kneeling down; but since I'm not a Christian
I didn't have their serenity of mind –
and I was trembling all over, and suffering;
and I was horrified, upset, deeply distressed.

Ah, don't smile; thirty-five years, just think –
winter, summer, night and day, thirty-five
years he's been living atop a pillar, martyring himself.
Before we were born – I'm twenty-nine years old,
and you, I daresay, are younger than I –

before we were born, imagine it,
Simeon went up onto the pillar
and ever since he's stayed there before his God.

Today I have no head for work. –
Except for this, Mebes: better if you say
that, whatever the other sophists say,
I myself acknowledge Lamo
as first among the poets of Syria.

THE BANDAGED SHOULDER

He said that he'd hit a wall, or that he'd fallen.
But probably there was another reason
for the wounded, bandaged shoulder.

With a rather sharp motion,
as he tried to take down from a shelf some
photographs that he wanted to see close up,
the bandage came undone and a little blood flowed.

I bound the shoulder up again, and over the binding
I lingered somewhat; for he wasn't in pain,
and I liked looking at the blood. Matter
of my love, is what that blood was.

When he left I found, in front of the chair,
a bloodied scrap of cloth, part of the bandage,
a scrap that looked like it should go straight into
        the trash;
and which I took upon my lips,
and which I kept for a long while –
the blood of love upon my lips.

[*1919*]

FROM THE DRAWER

I had in mind to place it on a wall of my room.

But the damp of the drawer damaged it.

I won't put this photograph in a frame.

I ought to have looked after it more carefully.

Those lips, that face –
ah if only for a day, only for an
hour their past would return.

I won't put this photograph in a frame.

I'll endure looking at it, damaged as it is.

Besides, even if it weren't damaged,
it would be annoying to be on guard lest some
word, some tone of voice betrayed –
if they ever questioned me about it.

THE REGIMENT OF PLEASURE

Do not speak of guilt, do not speak of responsibility. When the Regiment of Pleasure passes by, with music and flags; when the senses quiver and tremble, whoever stands apart is foolish and impertinent: whoever does not rush to join the good crusade, marching toward the conquest of pleasures and of passions.

All the laws of morals – as ill-considered as they are ill-constructed – are naught and cannot stand fast even for a moment, when the Regiment of Pleasure passes by accompanied by music and by flags.

Do not let a single shadowy virtue stop you. Do not believe that a single obligation binds you. Your duty is to give in, give in always to your longings, which are the most perfect creations of perfect gods. Your duty is to fall in, a faithful soldier, with simplicity of heart, when the Regiment of Pleasure passes by accompanied by music and by flags.

Do not shut yourself inside your house and deceive yourself with theories of justice, with the superstitions about reward held by ill-made societies. Do not say, My toil is worth so much, and so much I'm due to enjoy. Since life is an inheritance and you had nothing to do to earn it, so an inheritance, too, must Pleasure necessarily be. Do not shut yourself inside your house; but keep the window open, completely open, so that you might hear the first sounds of the passing of the soldiers, when the Regiment of Pleasure arrives accompanied by music and by flags.

Do not be deceived by the blasphemers who tell you that this service is risky and toilsome. Service to Pleasure is a constant joy. It exhausts you, but it exhausts you with heavenly intoxications. And when at last you fall down in the street, even then your fate is to be envied. When your funeral procession passes by, the Shapes that your longings fashioned will cast lilacs and white roses on your coffin, and onto their shoulders the youthful Gods of Olympus will lift you, and they will entomb you in the Cemetery of the Ideal where the mausoleums of poetry gleam white.

SHIPS

From Imagination onto Paper. Difficult the passage, risky the sea. The distance seems short at first sight, and yet even so how great a journey it is, and how harmful sometimes to the ships that undertake it.

The first sort of damage stems from the exceedingly fragile nature of the merchandise that the ships transport. In the marketplaces of the Imagination, the greatest number and the most beautiful of the objects are created of delicate glasses and porcelains translucent, and even with all the care in the world many shatter on the journey, and many shatter when they are unloaded ashore. All of the damage of this sort is irreparable, since it is out of the question for the ship to turn back and take aboard objects of comparable quality. It is impossible to find the same shop that sold them. The marketplaces of the Imagination have shops that are grand and opulent, but not of any great duration. Their transactions are brief, they dispose of their merchandise swiftly, and they are immediately liquidated. It is very rare for a ship to return and find the same exporters of the same goods.

Another sort of damage stems from the capacities of the ships themselves. They set out from the harbors of the prosperous mainlands heavy with cargo, and then when they find themselves upon the open sea they are forced to toss away a part of the cargo in order to save the whole. Hence virtually no ship manages to deliver intact precisely as many treasures as it had taken aboard. Those that were tossed away are, to be sure, the goods of lesser value, but sometimes it happens that sailors, in their great haste, make a mistake and toss into the sea some articles of great value.

Upon their arrival at the white harbor of paper, new sacrifices are required once again. The customs officials come and examine one item and ponder whether they should send the cargo back; they deny permission for another item to be unloaded; and of certain objects only a small quantity is admitted. The country has its laws. Not all goods have free entry and smuggling is strictly forbidden. The importation of wine is prohibited, since the lands from which the ships come make wines and spirits from grapes that grow and mature in more generous climates. The customs officials have no desire at all for these beverages. They are extremely intoxicating. They are not suitable for all heads. Besides there is an association in this country that has the monopoly on wines. It manufactures liquids having the color of wine and the taste of water, and you can drink them all day long without getting giddy in the slightest. It is an old association. It enjoys an excellent reputation, and its shares are always over-valued.

But we should be happy that the ships put into harbor; should be so even with all of those sacrifices.

For when all is said and done, thanks to great vigilance and great care, the number of objects shattered or cast overboard during the duration of the voyage is limited. Also, while the laws of the country and the customs regulations are oppressive in many respects, they are not completely restrictive, and a great part of the cargo is, in fact, unloaded. And the customs officials are not infallible, and various of the prohibited articles get through, inside deceptive containers which have been labeled one way on the outside but contain something else within, and several fine wines are imported for select drinking parties.

There is something else that is more distressing still; more distressing still. Sometimes certain enormous ships pass by, with décors of coral and with ebony masts, with tremendous white and scarlet banners flying, filled with treasure, and do not even approach the harbor either because all of the goods that they carry are forbidden or because the harbor does not have sufficient depth to receive them. And so they continue along on their course. A following wind breathes upon their silken sails, the sun glazes the brilliance of their golden prows, and they move away tranquilly and magnificently, move away forever from us and from our narrow harbor.

Fortunately they are very rare, those ships. Barely two or three do we see in all our lives. And we forget them quickly. As radiant as the sight of them is, so swift is the forgetting of them. And when a few years have passed, if some day – while we sit inertly looking at the light or listening to the silence – there should by chance return to our mind's ear some rousing stanzas, we do not recognize them at first and we torment our memory in order to recall where we heard them before. After a great deal of effort the ancient recollection wakens and we recall that those stanzas are from the hymn that the sailors were chanting, beautiful as the heroes of the *Iliad*, when the grand, the heavenly ships passed by and proceeded on their way going – who knows where.

From

THE UNFINISHED
POEMS
(1918–1932)

THE ITEM IN THE PAPER

A reference had been made, as well, to blackmail.
And here again the newspaper emphasized
its complete and utter contempt for depraved,
POEMS 1918–1932

Contempt ... And grieving inwardly he
recalled an evening from the year before
which they had spent together, in a room
that was half hotel, half brothel: afterward
they didn't meet again – not even in the street.
Contempt ... And he recalled the sweet
lips, and the white, the exquisite,
the sublime flesh that he hadn't kissed enough.

Melancholy, on the tram, he read the item.

At eleven at night the corpse was found
on the jetty. It wasn't clear
that foul play had been involved. The newspaper
expressed its pity, but, as usual,
it displayed its complete contempt
for the depraved way of life of the victim.

[*May 1918*]   201

IT MUST HAVE BEEN THE SPIRITS

It must have been the spirits that I drank last night,
it must have been that I was drowsing, I'd been tired
    all day long.

The black wooden column vanished before me,
with the ancient head; and the dining-room door,
and the armchair, the red one; and the little settee.
In their place came a street in Marseille.
And freed now, unabashed, my soul
appeared there once again and moved about,
with the form of a sensitive, pleasure-bent youth –
the dissolute youth: that too must be said.

It must have been the spirits that I drank last night,
it must have been that I was drowsing, I'd been tired
    all day long.

My soul found some ease; the poor thing, it's
always constrained by the weight of the years.

My soul found some ease and appeared to me
in a pleasant little street in Marseille,
with the form of the happy, dissolute youth
who never felt ashamed, not he, certainly.

AND ABOVE ALL CYNEGIRUS

Because he is of a great Italian house,
because he is, also, twenty years of age,
and because this is what they do in the great
    Greek world,
he came to Smyrna to learn rhetoric,
and to perfect his knowledge of their tongue.

And today he's listening, without
paying any attention at all, to the renowned sophist
who's speaking on Athens; who gesticulates,
and gets carried away, and tells the tale
of Miltiades, and the glorious battle of Marathon.
He's thinking about the drinking party he'll
    attend tonight;
and his imagination reveals to him a delicate face,
cherished lips that he's impatient to kiss . . .
He's thinking about how well he's doing here.
But his money's running out. And in a few months
he'll be going back to Rome. And he remembers
how many debts he's got there. And that the ordeal
of dodging payments will start all over again,
of finding means to live in a suitable style
(he is of a great Italian house).
Old man Fulvius's will —
ah, if only he could see it. If only he knew

how much he'll be getting from that old bugger
(two years, maybe three; he can't last longer!).
Will he leave him half, or a third? It's true
that he's already paid his debts twice before.

The sophist, very deeply moved,
pratically in tears, is talking about Cynegirus.

ON THE JETTY

Intoxicating night, in the dark, on the jetty.
And afterward in the little room at the tawdry
hotel – where we gave ourselves completely to our
      unwholesome passion; hour
after hour, again and again to "our own" love –
until the new day glistened on the windowpanes.

This evening the shape of the night resembles –
has revived in me – a night of the distant past.

Without any moon, extremely dark
(an advantage). Night of our encounter
on the jetty; at a great
distance from the cafés and the bars.

[*April 1920*]

AFTER THE SWIM

Naked, both of them, as they emerged from the sea at
    the Samian
shore; from the pleasure of the swim
(a blazing summer's day).
They were slow getting dressed, they were sorry
    to cover
the beauty of their sculpted nudity
which harmonized so well with the comeliness of
    their faces.

Ah the ancient Greeks were men of taste,
to represent the loveliness of youth
absolutely nude.

He wasn't completely wrong, poor old Gemistus
(let Lord Andronicus and the patriarch suspect him if
    they like),
in wanting us, telling us to become pagan once again.
My faith, the holy one, is always firmly pious –
but you can see what Gemistus was saying, to a point.

On young people at that time the teaching of
Georgius Gemistus had great influence,
who was most wise and exceedingly eloquent;
and an advocate of Hellenic education.

206   [*June 1921*]

BIRTH OF A POEM

One night when the beautiful light of the moon
poured into my room . . . imagination, taking
something from life: some very scanty thing –
a distant scene, a distant pleasure –
brought a vision all its own of flesh,
a vision all its own to a sensual bed . . .

THE PHOTOGRAPH

Looking at the photograph of a chum of his,
at his beautiful youthful face
(lost forever more; – the photograph
was dated 'Ninety-two),
the sadness of what passes came upon him.
But he draws comfort from the fact that at least
he hadn't let – they hadn't let any foolish shame
get in the way of their love, or make it ugly.
To the "degenerates," "obscene" of the imbeciles
their sensual sensibility paid no heed.

REMORSE

Talk about it, this remorse, to make it easier –
it's genuine to be sure, but dangerously one-sided.
Don't cling to the past and torment yourself so much.
Don't give so much importance to yourself.
The wrong you did was smaller than you
imagine; much smaller.
The goodness that has brought you this remorse now
was secreted inside you even then.
Look how some circumstance that suddenly
comes back to your memory explains
the reason for an action that had hardly seemed
commendable to you, but now can be excused.
Don't count too absolutely on your memory;
you've forgotten much – different odds and ends –
that would have been excuse enough.

And don't presume you knew the man you wronged
so very well. He surely had joys you didn't know of;
perhaps those aren't even scratches – what you
imagine (out of ignorance of his life)
are the dreadful wounds that you had given him.

Don't count on your feeble memory.
Temper your remorse, which is always
so one-sidedly against you, it's casuistry.

[October 1925]

CRIME

The money was divvied up for us by Stavros.
The best lad in our group,
clever, strong, and beautiful beyond imagining.
The ablest; even though, apart from me
(I was twenty years old), he was the youngest.
I daresay he wasn't quite twenty-three.

Three hundred pounds was the amount that we stole.
He kept, as his fair share, half of it.

But now, at eleven at night, we were planning
how to help him get away tomorrow morning,
before the police found out about the crime.
It wasn't minor: aggravated burglary.

We were inside a cellar.
A basement that was very safe.
Once a plan for his escape had been arranged,
the other three left us, me and Stavros;
we agreed that they'd come back at five o'clock.

There was a tattered mattress on the ground.
Worn out we both collapsed. And what with the
        emotional
upset, and the weariness,

and the anxiety about his running away
the next day – I barely realized: didn't fully realize
that this was, perhaps, the last time I'd lie near him.

In the papers of a poet this was found.
It does have a date, but it's difficult to read.
The *one* is barely visible; then *nine*, then
one; the fourth number looks like *nine*.

OF THE SIXTH OR SEVENTH CENTURY

It's very interesting and moving,
the Alexandria of the sixth century, or early in
    the seventh
before the coming of the mighty Arab nation.
She still speaks Greek, officially;
perhaps without much verve, yet, as is only fitting,
she speaks our language still.
Throughout the Greek world it's destined to
    fade away;
but here it's still holding up as best it can.

It's not unnatural if we have looked upon
this particular era so feelingly,
we who now have once more borne
the sound of Greek speech back to her soil.

ABANDONMENT

He was far too tasteful and far too clever,
a young man of very good society, too,
to play the fool, to act as if he thought
that his abandonment was some great tragedy.
After all when his friend had said to him, "We two
will have love forever" – both he who said it,
and he who heard it, knew it for a cliché.
One night after the picture-show, and the ten
minutes they stayed at the bar, a longing
kindled in their eyes and in their blood
and they went off together, and someone said "forever."

Anyway, their "forever" lasted three years.
Far too often it lasts for less.

He was far too elegant, and far too clever,
to take the matter tragically;
and far too beautiful – both face and body –
for his carnal vanity to be touched at all.

[*May 1930*]

NOTHING ABOUT THE
LACEDAEMONIANS

Certainly you ought to love sincerity
and serve it.
Still, don't overdo it, knowing you'll very likely
reach a point where sincerity won't do.
It's nice; and my, what a splendid feeling.
You'll express yourself honorably and sincerely
on many matters, and you'll be of help.
Rightly they will praise you: what a sincere fellow!
But put some water in your wine: don't presume
since (as you know) "Nothing about the
        Lacedaemonians."

COMPANY OF FOUR

The money that they make   certainly isn't honest.
But they're clever lads,   these four, and they have found
a way to make it work   and stay clear of the police.
Apart from being cunning,   they're extremely strong.
Because one pair is joined   by the bond of pleasure.
The other two are joined   by the bond of pleasure.
Dressed extremely well   as is fitting for
such good-looking lads;   the theatres and the bars,
and their automobile,   sometimes a little trip –
there's nothing that they lack.

The money that they make   certainly isn't honest:
now and then they fear   that someone will get hurt,
that they might go to jail.   But look, you see how Love
has a power that   can take their filthy money
and make it into something   gleaming, innocent.

Money – none of them   wants it for himself,
wants it selfishly.   None of them counts it out
greedily, boorishly;   they never even notice
if this one's carrying less,   or that one's got a lot.
They share their money out   so that they can be
elegantly dressed,   and spend it lavishly,
so they can make their life   tasteful, as is fitting

for such good-looking lads   so they can help
                                        their friends
and then – this is their system –   forget just what
                                        they gave.

AGELAUS

At the conference of Naupactus Agelaus
said what was only right. Fight no more wars
Greek against Greek. The looming struggle
is drawing nearer to us. Either Carthage
or Rome will be the victor, and afterward
will turn in our direction. O King
Philip, pray consider all the Greeks your own.
If you yearn for wars, prepare yourself
to face whoever's victor over Italy.
It's no longer the time for us to fight each other.
O King Philip, be the savior of Greece.

Words of wisdom. But they weren't heeded.
In the terrible, accursed days
of Cynoscephalae, of Magnesia, of Pydna,
many among the Greeks would recollect
those words of wisdom, which they didn't heed.

[*April 1932*]

NOTES

PUBLISHED POEMS

Poems 1905–1915

THE SATRAPY (p.20). **Satrapy** was the technical term given to the large administrative districts into which the Persian Empire was divided. **Susa** was the capital of Persia under the Achaemenid dynasty, which ruled Persia from the mid-seventh century B.C. until the death of Darius III in 330 B.C., following his defeat in battle by Alexander the Great. **Artaxerxes** was the name of several important Persian monarchs. The reference to Artaxerxes strongly suggests that the poet had, to some extent, been inspired by the later history of the 5th-century B.C. Athenian politician Themistocles (ca. 528–462 B.C.), who, after leading Athens to important victories over the Persians, was forced to leave Athens and eventually escaped to Persia, where he was welcomed by the king, Artaxerxes I. Nonetheless, Cavafy, in one of his unpublished "Self-Commentaries," asserted that the addressee of this poem is meant to be an artist or even a scientist, and not a public figure: "The poet is not necessarily thinking of Themistocles or Demaratos or any other political character ... the person intended is entirely symbolic..."

IDES OF MARCH. (p.22) Julius **Caesar** was assassinated on the **Ides** (the 15th) of March, 44 B.C. As Caesar made his way that morning to the Senate, where he hoped to hear himself declared King of Rome, a Greek scholar called **Artemidorus** tried to place a letter into his hand warning him of the plot to kill him, but was rebuffed.

THE GOD ABANDONS ANTONY (p.24). The title, in classical Greek, is a quotation from Plutarch's *Life of Antony*, where Plutarch describes the last night of Marc Antony's life, after his troops had deserted him and all Alexandria knew that Antony's cause was totally lost: "During this night ... while the city was quiet and dispirited because of fear and the anticipation of what was coming, suddenly there was heard the harmonious sound of all sorts of instruments, and the shouting of a crowd, together with revelry and satiric leaping about, as if a procession were leaving the city in a great tumult ... It seemed to those interpreting this sign that the god to whom Antony used to most liken himself, and dedicate himself [i.e., Dionysus], was now deserting him."

THEODOTUS (p.25). **Theodotus** of Chios, a rhetorician at the court of the Ptolemies in Alexandria, is said to have urged the murder of **Pompey** (Gnaius Pompeius Magnus, 106–48 B.C.), the powerful rival of Julius Caesar. Pompey had once ruled Rome alongside Caesar, but his relationship with his one-time colleague disintegrated, and eventually the two met in a pitched battle at Pharsalus, where Pompey was defeated in 48. He then fled to Egypt, where he was stabbed to death on landing there, in September 48 B.C. It was at the foot of a statue of Pompey, erected in the Roman Senate, that Caesar himself was assassinated.

ITHACA (p.27). An early version of this poem was written in 1894; the present version was composed in October 1910 and published in November of the following year. In Homer's *Odyssey*, the monsters that Odysseus encounters on his ten-year voyage home from Troy include man-eating giants called

Laestrygonians, as well as Polyphemus, a **Cyclops** (another race of cannibalistic giants) whom Odysseus blinds in a famous episode recounted in book 9 of the poem. Because Polyphemus is actually a son of the sea-god **Poseidon**, Poseidon vengefully pursues Odysseus thereafter, causing storms and shipwrecks and punishing those who help the hero on his way home. The poverty of the rocky island kingdom of Ithaca was proverbial.

KING DEMETRIUS (p.31). **Demetrius Poliorcetes** ("the Besieger of Cities") assumed the throne of Macedonia in the tumultuous years of dynastic struggle soon after the death of Alexander the Great. Demetrius was eventually expelled from Macedonia, and his final struggle to maintain power ended in disgrace when his troops, tired of serving his overweening imperial ambitions and taste for luxury, deserted him to join the enemy leader, **Pyrrhus**. The epigraph of the poem, in Classical Greek, is taken from Plutarch's *Life of Demetrius*, and describes Demetrius's departure from his camp after it became obvious that his men were deserting him *en masse*.

ALEXANDRIAN KINGS (p.33). In a propagandistic ceremony known as the "Donations" (34 B.C.), Marc Antony promoted the imperialistic claims of his alliance with **Cleopatra**. The elaborate titles given to her children, while wholly symbolic, suggest the scope of the couple's ambitions: all of the lands once ruled by Alexander the Great were, at least in name, distributed to the young royals. **Alexander** Helios and **Ptolemy** Philadelphus were Cleopatra's children by Antony; as his nickname suggests, **Caesarion**'s father was Julius Caesar, who had been Cleopatra's lover.

PHILHELLENE. (p.35) In this dramatic monologue, a princeling who rules some unnamed but clearly remote Eastern possession of the Roman empire – **Zagros** is the major mountain range of present-day Iran, and in ancient times constituted the border between Media and Mesopotamia; and **Phráata** was the summer seat of the Parthian kings – issues orders for new coinage to be struck.

THE STEPS (p.36). The Roman Emperor **Nero** (37–68 A.D.) was the son of Agrippina the Younger, a great-granddaughter of Augustus, who was murdered in 59 A.D. at her son's instructions, and of Gnaeus Domitius Ahenobarbus, a member of the distinguished old clan of the **Ahenobarbi**. In Roman religion, **lares** were tutelary deities associated with the spirits of the family ancestors; typically a Roman house contained a private chapel or shrine called the *lararium*, inside of which were small images of these deities. Vengeance for the crime of matricide was, in Greek mythology, thought to be the province of creatures called Erinyes – "Furies" – winged apparitions who are described in Aeschylus's *Oresteia* as having dog-like faces dripping with blood, and who pursued matricides and drove them mad.

DANGEROUS (p.39). The dramatic date of this poem is the joint reign of **Constans** and **Constantius II**, the two sons of Constantine the Great, the emperor who officially made Christianity the supreme religion of the Roman Empire (d. 337 A.D.). By this time the Roman empire had been divided into Eastern and Western regions, each ruled by an emperor bearing the title of *augustus*.

MANUEL COMNENUS (p.40). The Byzantine emperor **Manuel I Comnenus** (born ca. 1120) transformed the austere and pious court of his devout father into a center of glittering festivity, with tournaments borrowed from Western Europe. After his army was shattered by the Turks at the battle of Myriocephalum in 1176, he was said never to have laughed or smiled again. He died on September 24, 1180.

Poems 1916–1918

CAESARION (p.57). **Caesarion** ("Little Caesar") was the son of Julius Caesar and Cleopatra. A year after the suicides of Antony and Cleopatra in 30 B.C., Octavian (later Augustus) had the teenaged Caesarion put to death; as he gave the order for the murder, he is said to have complained sardonically of the dangers of *polykaisariê*, "too many Caesars." The Greek word is a punning allusion to a passage in the *Iliad* (2. 203–6) in which Odysseus, berating some mutinous troops, complains that too many commanders, *polykoiraniê*, is a bad thing.

NERO'S DEADLINE (p.59) As the cruelties and egomaniacal excesses of the emperor **Nero** worsened, a plot to overthrow him was instigated by C. Julius Vindex. (Among those excesses was Nero's ludicrous concert tour of Greece – known to the Romans as the province of **Achaea** – in the year 67, when he "liberated" the province.) Vindex invited the popular governor of Spain, Servius Sulpicius **Galba** (3 B.C.–69 A.D.), a member of an extremely distinguished aristocratic family, to join the conspiracy. Galba eventually marched on Rome, and after Nero's suicide in 68 became emperor.

IN THE MONTH OF HATHOR (p. 65). Here Cavafy has re-created the appearance of a scholarly transcription of a tomb inscription. In such transcriptions, letters that are missing or illegible in the original (which can, however, be inferred from context) are rendered in brackets, so as to distinguish between what is actually legible and what is intelligible. **Athyr** is the poet's transcription of Hathor, the name of the cow-headed Egyptian goddess whose eponymous month came late in the autumn. In Greek, the letters **KAPPA** and **ZETA** (KZ), taken together, also represent the number 27, i.e., the age of the deceased.

Poems 1919–1932

YOUNG MEN OF SIDON (400 A.D.) (p.85). **Sidon** was an important commercial city of Phoenicia, located on the coast of present-day Lebanon; in antiquity it was a major producer of luxury goods, such as purple dye, and also of glass. The date of **400 A.D.** is suggestive, marking as it does a historical moment not long after the triumph of Christianity in the Roman Empire, and not long before the advent of the barbarians. **Meleager**, **Crinagoras** and **Rhianus** were poets known for their epigrams. The great playwright Aeschylus (ca. 525–456 B.C.) composed his own verse epitaph, which makes no mention of his tragedies, referring only to his service in the Persian Wars of 490 B.C. The Persian generals at the Battle of Marathon, in which Aeschylus fought, were **Datis** and **Artaphernes**.

DARIUS (p.88). **Darius the Great** of Persia (521–486 B.C.) was the king who instigated the so-called Persian Wars with the

Greeks from 490 to 479 B.C., famous for the battles of Marathon, Thermopylae, and Salamis, which marked the Greeks' improbable victory over the far larger Persian forces. **Mithridates VI Eupatôr Dionysus** ("the Great") was the last independent ruler of Pontus, a kingdom constituting the northern part of Asia Minor and extending as far south as the area known as **Cappadocia**. Born about 132 B.C., Mithridates waged three major wars against the Romans; the event described in the poem is most likely the onset of the Third Mithridatic War, in 74 B.C. The name of the fictional poet in this poem, **Phernazes**, is Persian.

FROM THE SCHOOL OF THE RENOWNED PHILOSOPHER (p.93). **Ammonius Saccas** (d. 242 A.D.), "the Socrates of Neoplatonism," was an Alexandrian Christian, famous as the teacher of two crucially important figures in Christian philosophy, Origen and Plotinus. Plotinus – presumably a fellow-student of the vain and shallow fictional subject of this poem – maintained that the soul stood halfway between pure mind and the inferior flesh, and that moral choices were, therefore, choices between the aspirations of the former and the primitive urges of the latter.

THOSE WHO FOUGHT ON BEHALF OF THE ACHAEAN LEAGUE (p.95). The title of the poem, in Classical Greek, purports to be from an epigram written (as the last lines indicate) during the reign of the Hellenistic Egyptian king Ptolemy IX (ca. 141–81 B.C.), contemptuously nicknamed *Lathyros*, "**Chickpea**." The bloody family politics of the Ptolemies establishes an ironic frame for the idealistic praise in the preceding lines for the **Achaean League**. The League, an association of Greek city-states formed in 280 B.C., was the chief Greek political power during the period that saw the rise and eventual triumph of Rome. In 146 B.C. the League's forces, serving under the incompetent commanders **Diaeus** and **Critolaus**, were defeated by the Romans.

THEATRE OF SIDON (400 A.D.) (p.98). "Those who wear gray clothes" is a reference to Christians.

OF COLORED GLASS (p.101). After the Civil War of 1341–47, **John VI Cantacuzenus** was crowned emperor of Byzantium in the **Blachernae** Palace in Constantinople in May, 1347. The "detail" to which Cavafy refers is related by the Byzantine historian Nicephorus Gregoras who, in a long passage devoted to the emperor's coronation, describes the sorry state of the imperial household after the deprivations of the Civil War (during which John's arch-enemy, the widowed empress **Anna of Savoy**, emptied the treasuries and sold off the palace treasures in order to finance her schemes). **Andronicus Asen**, the father of John's wife, **Irene**, had betrayed John early in the Civil War, joining forces with Anna and her cronies.

ON THE ITALIAN SEASHORE (p.103). The poem alludes to the aftermath of the Roman triumph over the Greek forces of the Achaean League in 146 B.C. The Roman general Mummius sacked Corinth as an example to Greeks contemplating future resistance. The population of the famously luxurious and pleasure-loving city was put to the sword, and the city was stripped of its great treasures, which were then shipped to Italy. **Italiote** refers to an ethnically Greek inhabitant of Southern Italy – a person of typically Cavafian mixed identities and loyalties.

IN A MUNICIPALITY OF ASIA MINOR (p.106). Julius Caesar's heir Octavian (later Augustus Caesar) resoundingly defeated the combined forces of Antony and Cleopatra at the battle of Actium in 31 B.C.

PRIEST OF THE SERAPEUM (p.107). The temple of the god Serapis, known as the **Serapeum**, was considered one of the wonders of the world. Imported to Egypt in around 300 B.C., worship of Serapis, a hybrid god who combined many aspects of existing Greco-Roman and Egyptian deities, was widespread throughout the Mediterranean and in the cities of the Eastern Roman Empire. The Serapeum was destroyed by a Christian mob in 391 A.D.

JULIAN AND THE ANTIOCHENES (p.110). Cavafy wrote more poems about the apostate emperor **Julian** (331?–363 A.D.) than about any other historical figure. During his controversial reign, Julian tried to re-establish pagan worship in the Roman empire, not long after it had been Christianized by his uncle, Constantine the Great. From July 362 A.D. to March 363, when he went off on the campaign against Persia in which he would perish, Julian resided at Antioch, one of the great cities of Asia Minor. There, his restoration of numerous pagan shrines and temples and desecration of Christian shrines hardly endeared him to the Antiochenes, and his ostentatious asceticism and arcane, anti-populist philosophical program made him an object of ridicule in the eyes of the notoriously pleasure-loving local population. Julian wrote a diatribe against the locals (from which the epigraph of this poem is taken); in it, he quotes the Antiochenes' wry observation that, compared to Julian, neither his predecessor, the Christian

229

emperor Constantius (represented by the letter *K*, the first letter of his name as spelled in Greek) nor Christ himself (represented by the letter *X*, "chi," the first letter of the Greek spelling of *Christ*) had harmed their city.

POTENTATE FROM WESTERN LIBYA (p.118). **Libya** was the Greek name for the entire continent of Africa; it is difficult to know where, precisely, Cavafy's fictitious potentate, a short-term visitor to Hellenistic Alexandria, is supposed to come from.

MYRES: ALEXANDRIA IN 340 A.D. (p.120). This is the longest poem that Cavafy published. The specificity of the date in the title situates Myres' death during the tumultuous joint reign of Constans and Constantius, the sons of Constantine the Great (the setting of "Dangerous," p. 39). It was a period marked by internecine divisions within the state and within the Church, and hence the ideal setting for the poem's delineation of the speaker's growing awareness of a division between himself, a pagan, and his dead beloved, a Christian.

COME NOW, KING OF THE LACEDAEMONIANS (p.125). The Spartan king **Cleomenes III** (ca. 260–219 B.C.) was a social reformer who – inspired, it would seem, by dreams of restoring Sparta to the greatness she enjoyed during her Archaic and Classical past – drastically reorganized the Spartan state during the 220s B.C., and embarked on ambitious military campaigns. As part of his strategy, he sought an alliance with the Egyptian king Ptolemy III, who agreed on the condition that the Spartan king's mother, **Cratesicleia**, as well as his children, be sent to Alexandria as political hostages. Both she and her grandchildren were executed by Ptolemy's successor.

INTERRUPTION (p.142). The poem refers to two myths in which mortals disastrously intrude on processes meant to render human children immortal. In one tale, **Demeter**, running amok on Earth in her grief for her ravished daughter Persephone, eventually comes to the town of **Eleusis**, where, disguised as an old woman, she ends up working in the house of the king as a nurse to his infant son. There she begins the arcane process of transforming the baby into an immortal by sticking him each night among the glowing embers of the hearth-fire. One night, his mother, the queen **Metaneira**, enters the room and interrupts Demeter, who in a rage hurls the boy to the ground and stalks out of the royal palace. In another myth, the nymph **Thetis** attempted to render her son, Achilles, virtually immortal by dipping him in the terrible waters of the river Styx, but (in Cavafy's version) is interrupted by her husband, **Peleus**, with the result that the boy's ankle is left vulnerable.

THERMOPYLAE (p.143). The battle of **Thermopylae** (the name of a narrow mountain pass in north-central Greece that controlled access to the cities to the south), was one of the most important battles of the Persian Wars (490–479 B.C.), in which the Persian Empire, first under Darius the Great and then under his son Xerxes, attempted to subjugate the cities of mainland Greece. In September, 480 B.C., a Greek force of between six and seven thousand troops bravely held the pass for two days, until a local man called **Ephialtes** betrayed them, showing the Persians an alternative route round the pass. After this, nearly all the Greeks withdrew or panicked, leaving about three hundred men behind, mostly Spartans, who heroically fought a rear-guard action until the last man had been killed; this action gave the departing force time enough to leave the vicinity safely.

CHE FECE . . . IL GRAN RIFIUTO (p.144). The title is a quotation from Dante's *Inferno*, Canto 3. As Vergil and Dante pass through the gates of Hell they behold a long line of souls who have been damned for never having committed either to good or to evil; among them is that of Pope Celestine V, a saintly and ascetic hermit who, having been elected to the papacy at the age of eighty, in 1294, resigned the office only a few months later. This extraordinary rejection of the Holy See (Celestine was he "who made the great refusal," *fece il gran rifiuto*) earned Dante's contempt primarily because it paved the way for the election of Boniface VIII, a pope for whom the Italian poet had a special loathing.

WAITING FOR THE BARBARIANS (p.147). This poem at first seems to be among the strongest expressions, on the part of the younger Cavafy, of the pessimistic lassitude and resistance to the idea of progress typical of the Decadents. And yet the poet left an interesting note, dating to a period of intense re-evaluation of his work (1903–1904), that calls for a more complicated reading of this poem: "Possible situation; not likely; not my own prediction. My own notion concerning the future is more optimistic. Anyway, the poem is not at odds with my own optimistic notion; it can be taken as an episode in the progress towards Good." The note suggests a certain impatience with the facile attitude of ennui that was characteristic of the Decadents whom he liked to mimic as a young poet, and which, as he evolved into his mature phase, seemed to him to be too unsubtle and lacking in intellectual nuance.

REPUDIATED POEMS

OEDIPUS (p.159). The French painter Gustave Moreau (1826–1898) exhibited his painting of the confrontation between Oedipus and the Sphinx in 1864. Cavafy's poem is based on a description of the painting that appeared in a journal. In myth, Oedipus – at first acclaimed for solving the riddle of the Sphinx, later reviled when it is revealed that he had killed his father and married his mother – wandered, a beggar, from city to city after blinding himself, and in great old age came to the sacred grove of the Furies at **Colonus**, a suburb of Athens. There, after a series of final confrontations with his rebellious sons and loyal daughters, Oedipus was purged of his guilt, and after dying was elevated to semi-divine status.

HORACE IN ATHENS (p.161). **Horace** (Quintus Horatius Flaccus, 65–8 B.C.) was the greatest lyric poet of Roman literature. His intimate familiarity with Greek literature, so evident throughout his distinctive work, was polished during the years in his early twenties when he studied, as well-off Roman youths often did, in **Athens**. It was in Athens that the youthful Horace had his one bruising experience with high political passions and grandiose world events: after the twenty-year-old student learned of Julius Caesar's assassination, he joined the doomed republican forces of Cassius and Brutus against those of Octavian. Horace barely escaped from the battle of Philippi with his life, slinking back to Rome "with clipped wings," as he wrote in one of his poems.

THE TARENTINES HAVE THEIR FUN (p.162). In the late 280s B.C., Rome had been consolidating its power throughout

Southern Italy, attacking a number of Greek colonies there –
a state of affairs that caused no little alarm in Tarentum, then
the largest Greek colony in South Italy. In the summer of 282
B.C. the Tarentines, who happened to be gathered in their sea-
side theater, saw a number of Roman ships sailing into their
harbor. This was a violation of an agreement between the two
cities: the Tarentines sent some ships to attack the Roman
fleet, and the Greeks were successful in sinking several of the
Roman ships and killing a number of sailors. The outraged
Romans sent a delegation of officials demanding reparations,
but they had the bad luck to arrive in the autumn, during the
local Dionysiac festival, which was also held in the theater.
The Romans were led to the stage of the theater and asked
to state their purpose, and when the chief envoy, the senator
L. Postumius, addressed the crowd, his awkward Greek was
ridiculed by the Tarentines, one of whom later threw garbage
at the Roman's toga. "Laugh now," he is said to have declared
to them then, "but this toga will not be cleansed until it is
washed in your blood." The Romans later attacked and plun-
dered Tarentum.

UNPUBLISHED POEMS

TO STEPHANOS SKILITSIS (p.165). **Skilitsis** was one of
Cavafy's two closest friends from the days when he, his
widowed mother, and his two immediately older brothers,
John and Paul, returned to Alexandria from England in the
autumn of 1877. Skilitsis – who in an 1885 letter to the future
poet teasingly chided Cavafy for not sharing details of his
private life – died on April 8, 1886, at the age of nineteen.

Cavafy saved a copy of the death notice that appeared in the Alexandrian paper *Telegraphos*.

"NOUS N'OSONS PLUS CHANTER LES ROSES." (p.166). The title of the poem is a quotation from "Printemps Oublié" ("Forgotten Spring") by René-François-Armand Sully Prudhomme (1839–1907), winner of the first Nobel Prize in Literature; the poem is preoccupied with the dangers of writing poetry on hackneyed themes.

JULIAN AT THE MYSTERIES (p.172). The inspiration for this poem is an episode from the youth of Julian the Apostate (331?–363 A.D.), the emperor who tried to re-establish pagan worship after Rome had been Christianized. At the age of twenty, Julian, who had been raised a Christian, was initiated into the Eleusinian Mysteries, the secret rites associated with the goddesses Demeter and Persephone that held out to true believers a promise of eternal life. Apparently Julian was so terrified by the flashing lights and other supernatural phenomena that were part of the pagan ceremony that he reflexively made the sign of the cross when he saw them.

POSEIDONIANS (p.183). The favorite theme of once-great civilizations that are ultimately superseded, and in particular of peripheral cultures eagerly trying to stake a claim to Hellenism, haunts this poem in a number of ways. The **Poseidonians** were the inhabitants of Poseidonia, a significant Greek colony in Italy, known under the Romans as Paestum. **Tyrrhenians** was the name by which the Greeks referred to the Etruscans, the indigenous people who inhabited the Italian peninsula until they too were effaced by the Romans (also called **Latins**). **Italiotes** refers to the Greek population of Southern Italy, which during the seventh and sixth centuries B.C. was heavily colonized by Greek settlers.

THEOPHILUS PALAEOLOGUS (p.187). On May 29, 1453, the Byzantine empire came to an end with the fall of Constantinople to the Ottoman sultan, Mehmet II. By that time, the capital city was virtually all that remained of the once-sprawling empire, and in the months leading up to the city's fall it was clear that resistance by the isolated forces of the last emperor, Constantine XI, could only achieve a symbolic status at best. During the climactic battle for the city, Constantine's cousin, **Theophilus Palaeologus**, a scholar and mathematician, is said to have fought alongside him and uttered the words *thélo thaneín mállon ê zên*, "I'd rather die than live," as he threw himself into the mêlée.

SIMEON (p.189). Saint **Simeon the Stylite**, who lived from the late fourth to the mid-fifth century A.D., was an ascetic Christian who gained renown for living on a small platform atop a pillar for thirty-seven years. Simeon was the object of an abiding fascination for Cavafy, and of a great admiration. "This great, this wonderful saint," the poet wrote, "is surely an object to be singled out in ecclesiastical history for admiration and study. He has been, perhaps, the only man who has dared to be really *alone*."

THE UNFINISHED POEMS

AND ABOVE ALL CYNEGIRUS (p.203). The title is a quotation from a treatise on oratory by the great satirist Lucian of Samosata (120–180? A.D.), in which the author lampooned the mania among contemporary authors for aping the style of Greek writers of six hundred years earlier. One of the clichés he singled out for ridicule was the invocation of the heroism of the Athenian soldier **Cynegirus**, brother of the playwright Aeschylus, who died at the battle of Marathon in 490 B.C. (in which the Greek troops were led by the Athenian general **Miltiades**).

AFTER THE SWIM (p.206). **Georgius Gemistus Plethon** (ca. 1355–1452) was a leading Byzantine scholar and a principal figure in the revival of Classical learning in Western Europe. A rare champion of the Platonic (as opposed to the far more prevalent Aristotelian) philosophical vision, he is said to have taken the additional surname *Plêthon*, an archaizing synonym for *gemistos*, "full," because it sounded like "Plato." His preference for Plato, perceived as a covert paganism, aroused the ire of church authorities. Eventually, his Aristotelian rival, Georgios Scholarios (eventually **Patriarch** of Constantinople) persuaded the emperor Manuel II Palaeologus to exile Gemistus; the order may have been carried out by Manuel's son, **Andronicus**. In his final work, the *Book of Laws*, an attempt to synthesize Neoplatonism and belief in the Olympian gods, the elderly Gemistus flatly stated that Zeus was the supreme god. The treatise was burned by Scholarios.

OF THE SIXTH OR SEVENTH CENTURY (p.212). In September of 642 A.D., having already conquered the Byzantine strongholds of Jerusalem, Antioch, Aleppo, Damascus, and a number of other cities in a series of stunning victories, Arab forces led by Amr Ibn-el-'Aas, the great general of the caliph Omar I, entered Alexandria. The conquerors were barely able to contain their admiration for the lavish capital: "The moonlight reflected from the white marble made the city so bright," one is reported to have marveled, "that a tailor could see to thread his needle without a lamp. No one entered the city without having a covering on his eyes to veil him from the glare of the plaster and marble." On the caliph's orders, the entire collection of the Library of Alexandria – except for the works of Aristotle – was burned as fuel to heat water for the public baths.

NOTHING ABOUT THE LACEDAEMONIANS (p.214). The title is Cavafy's paraphrase of the opening line of a message that accompanied 300 Persian panoplies sent by Alexander the Great to Athens to commemorate his victory over the forces of Darius III, the king of Persia. This line, typically for Greek communications of the time, constituted what we might today refer to as the "from" line: ALEXANDER, SON OF PHILIP, AND THE GREEKS EXCEPT FOR THE LACEDAEMONIANS." *Except for the Lacedaemonians* pointedly alludes to the fact that of the Greek states, only Sparta (also known as Lacedaemon) refused to join in Alexander's campaign against Persia, proudly unwilling, as they were, to serve under a non-Spartan general. And yet this ostensibly high-minded and nationalistic pride cost the militaristic Lacedaemonians dearly, since in refusing to join the Macedonian's expedition into Asia, they missed out on the greatest military conquests the world had ever seen.

238

AGELAUS (p.217). The Second Punic War (218–202 B.C.) between the expanding Roman Republic and its great rival in North Africa, Carthage, created a rare opportunity for the perennially warring Greek city states to band together and, united, to confront their common enemy to the west. After learning of the Carthaginians' devastating defeat of the Romans at Lake Trasimene in the north of Italy, in June 217, **Philip V** of Macedon (238–179 B.C.), the most powerful man on the Greek mainland, was persuaded that negotiations with the other Greek states would be advantageous, and a peace conference took place at the port city of **Naupactus**, on the Gulf of Corinth. Here, according to the historian Polybius, one of the delegates, **Agelaus**, gave a rousing speech in which he showed a prescient understanding for the necessity of a concerted Greek front against Rome. His advice was heeded, but within a few years Greek unity had, all too typically, become fragmented. Three devastating defeats of the Greek states by the Romans over the course of the next few decades – the battles of **Cynoscephalae**, in 197, of **Magnesia**, in 190, and of **Pydna**, in 168 – marked the end of Greek power in the Mediterranean.